Commission of Public Works

Commissioners of Public Works (Ireland) : fifty-seventh report with appendices

Commission of Public Works

Commissioners of Public Works (Ireland) : fifty-seventh report with appendices

ISBN/EAN: 9783741105739

Manufactured in Europe, USA, Canada, Australia, Japa

Cover: Foto ©ninafisch / pixelio.de

Manufactured and distributed by brebook publishing software
(www.brebook.com)

Commission of Public Works

Commissioners of Public Works (Ireland) : fifty-seventh report

with appendices

PUBLIC WORKS, IRELAND.

FIFTY-SEVENTH ANNUAL REPORT

OF THE

COMMISSIONERS OF PUBLIC WORKS

IN

IRELAND:

WITH

APPENDICES,

FOR THE YEAR 1888-89.

Presented to both Houses of Parliament by Command of Her Majesty.

DUBLIN:
PRINTED FOR HER MAJESTY'S STATIONERY OFFICE
BY
ALEXANDER THOM & CO. (LIMITED),

And to be purchased, either directly or through any Bookseller, from
EYRE and SPOTTISWOODE, East Harding-street, Fetter-lane, E.C., or 32, Abingdon-street,
Westminster, S.W.; or ADAM and CHARLES BLACK, 6, North Bridge, Edinburgh; or
HODGES, FIGGIS, and Co., 104, Grafton-street, Dublin.

1889.

[C.—5726.] *Price 6d.*

the University of

TABLE OF CONTENTS.

REPORT AND APPENDICES.

APPENDICES.

PUBLIC WORKS, IRELAND.

FIFTY-SEVENTH ANNUAL REPORT

OF THE

COMMISSIONERS OF PUBLIC WORKS IN IRELAND,

FOR THE YEAR 1888-89.

TO THE LORDS COMMISSIONERS OF HER MAJESTY'S TREASURY.

MAY IT PLEASE YOUR LORDSHIPS,

WE have the honour to submit our Fifty-seventh Annual Report on the several LOANS, VOTED, and MISCELLANEOUS services entrusted to our management, viz. :—

I. LOANS:

For Public Works under Acts 1 & 3 Wm. IV., c. 33, 40 & 41 Vic., c. 27, &c., embracing among others the following separate classes of loans :—

> Labourers' Dwellings in Towns Act, 1866, and Housing of the Working Classes Act, 1885.
> Glebe Loans.
> Public Health.
> River Drainage Works Act, 1863.
> River Drainage Maintenance.
> Lunatic Asylums Buildings.
> Reformatories.
> Labourers' (Ireland) Act, 1883.
> National School Teachers' Residences.
> Dispensary Houses.
> Non-Vested National Schools and Training Colleges.
> Industrial Schools (Ireland) Act, 1885.

Loans for Improvement of Lands, viz. :—
Drainage of Lands ; Erection of Farm Houses and Buildings ; Erection of Scutch Mills ; Erection of Dwellings for Agricultural Labourers ; Planting for Shelter.

Land Law (Ireland) Act, 1881, Loans to Tenants.
For most of the purposes enumerated in the preceding service.
Landlord and Tenant Act, 1870.
Loans under Relief of Distress Acts, 1880.

II. VOTED SERVICES :

Public Buildings, Ireland, viz. :—
Naval and Military ; State and Official Residences ; Civil Departments ; Legal Departments ; Metropolitan Police ; Royal Irish Constabulary ; Dundrum Criminal Lunatic Asylum ; Science and Art Department ; Public Education ; Royal University and Queen's Colleges ; Revenue Departments.

Royal Parks and Gardens :—
Phoenix Park ; St. Stephen's-green ; The Curragh of Kildare.

Royal Harbours :—
Kingstown ; Howth ; Donaghadee ; Dunmore ; Ardglass.

Inland Navigations :—
Tyrone ; Maigue ; Ulster Canal.
Royal University of Ireland Buildings.
Science and Art Buildings. New Museum and Library.
Ancient Monuments Protection Act, 45 & 46 Vic., c. 73.

III. MISCELLANEOUS OR NON-VOTED SERVICES :

Arterial Drainage Works.
Arterial Drainage, Maintenance and Increased Rents, and Railway Clauses Consolidation Act.
Fishery Piers and Harbours Acts, 1846 and 1883.
Fishery Piers and Harbours Maintenance.
Arklow and Kinsale Harbours.
Clare Slob Reclamation.
Shannon Navigation.
Boyne Navigation.
Irish Reproductive Loan Fund.

Sea and Coast Fisheries (Ireland) Loan Fund.
National Monuments and Ecclesiastical Ruins, 33 & 34 Vic., c. 46.
Post Road Repairs.
County Surveyors' Assistants.
Bridges, between Counties.
Limited Owners' Residences.
Arbitrations—For Railways and other Public Works.
Tramways and Light Railways (Ireland) Act, 1883.
Loans—Receiver's Account.

The following is an Abstract of Loans made by the Commissioners of Public Works, showing the
Amounts Remitted, and

No.	SERVICES	No. of Loans sanctioned on 31st March, 1889.	ADVANCED TO BORROWERS.		PRINCIPAL
			In the Year ended 31st March, 1889.	Total up to the 31st March, 1889.	In the Year on, etc. Paid
	I. Public Works Loans, 1 & 2 Wm. IV., c. 33, 40 & 41 Vic., c. 27 :—		£ s. d.	£ s. d.	£ s. d.
1	Loans to Grand Juries of Counties for Roads, Court-houses, &c.,	43	4,620 11 9	764,647 7 8	9,195 16 5
2	Local Boards—various works,	28	22,400 0 0	161,474 8 0	1,859 0 10
3	Roads and Bridges,	7	—	290,577 0 4	6,800 16 10
4	Inland Navigation,	5	4,500 0 0	179,697 8 3	921 7 0
5	Public Buildings—erection and completion,	2	—	70,500 0 0	7,084 16 6
6	Railways—in aid of construction,	33	84,770 0 0	1,174,290 10 11	89,466 1 9
7	Quarries, Mines, and Miscellaneous Purposes,	1	—	18,383 0 0	29 9 1
8	Harbours, Docks, &c.—in aid of construction,	26	3,918 0 0	504,129 5 1	8,067 16 3
9	Fishery Piers and Harbours—2 Vic., c. 5,	6	—	51,644 17 3	675 14 1
10	Reclamation of Waste Lands (Clare Sub.)—1 & 2 Wm. IV., c. 33,	1	1,550 0 0	130,641 0 0	—
11	Labourers' Dwellings in Towns—30 & 30 Vic., c. 44,	64	—	152,561 15 2	4,606 17 9
12	Housing of the Working Classes—46 & 46 Vic., c. 71,	65	19,285 0 0	137,619 0 0	4,457 9 0
13	Artisans' Dwellings—clearing unhealthy areas—38 & 39 Vic. c. 36,	6	—	61,000 0 0	3,796 13 4
14	Glebe Loans—erection or purchase of Glebe Houses, and purchase of Land—53 & 54 Vic., c. 112,	916	11,829 6 6	421,620 8 8	6,905 11 6
15	Public Health—Sanitary Works—27 & 30 Vic., c. 33, and 41 & 42 Vic., c. 52,	669	74,671 14 4	3,821,911 0 9	162,278 4 10
16	River Drainage Works—5 & 6 Vic., c. 89,	33	—	2,082,068 7 3	562 2 9
17	Do. 26 & 27 Vic., c. 88,	227	31,905 0 0	778,066 18 10	30,150 14 7
18	Maintenance of Drainage Works—29 & 30 Vic., c. 44, and 43 & 44 Vic., c. 14, sec. 19,	201	415 10 0	42,388 6 1	1,942 2 7
19	Public Works—37 Geo. III., c. 94,	3	—	491,444 19 9	—
20	Repairs of Post Roads and Bridges—6 & 7 Wm. IV., c. 116,	9	621 6 6	184,560 0 7	161 3 0
21	Land Improvement—Preliminary Expenses—10 Vic., c. 32, sec. 16,	1	1,000 0 0	62,000 0 0	617 4 1
22	Repairs of Fishery Piers—16 & 17 Vic., c. 136,	4	—	14,697 10 0	648 8 9
23	Maintenance of Navigation Works—19 & 20 Vic., c. 62,	—	—	2,464 0 0	—
24	Lunatic Asylums Buildings—erection of—1 & 2 Geo. IV., c. 33, &c.	178	28,836 6 4	1,425,649 7 6	23,806 14 0
25	Building Schools—37 Geo. III., c. 197,	3	—	30,296 5 7	13 11 1
26	Relief of Distress—Supply of Food and Fuel—43 Vic., c. 4,	3	—	14,796 8 0	346 0 0
27	Seed Supply—Purchase of Seed—43 Vic., c. 1,	44	—	647,342 11 10	12,071 1 3
28	Emigration (assisting)—45 & 46 Vic., c. 47,	30	—	11,706 3 10	718 7 9
29	Labourers' Acts—Erection of Cottages—46 & 47 Vic., c. 60, &c.	1,399	342,367 1 5	648,419 9 6	4,975 0 1
30	Loans to Landlords—for Improvement of Lands, &c.—10 Vic., c. 32 &c.,	3,053	31,771 4 5	7,951,725 3 10	90,661 3 0
31	National School Teachers' Residences—38 & 39 Vic., c. 96,	411	12,462 10 0	97,711 10 0	1,456 4 1
32	Dispensary Houses—43 & 44 Vic., c. 25,	62	6,708 0 0	66,951 0 0	3,509 7 7
33	Non-Vested Schools and Training Colleges—47 & 48 Vic., c. 52,	63	2,225 0 0	22,090 0 0	366 0 9
34	Loans to Tenants—for Improvement of Lands, 44 & 45 Vic., c. 49, c. 71,	6,220	33,541 0 5	645,250 0 0	21,546 18 9
35	Do. for Purchase of Holdings, 53 & 54 Vic., c. 48,	683	—	616,716 13 0	8,019 4 6
	Total Open Loan Services,	12,328	687,021 16 5	17,204,906 7 2	438,334 19 6
	Total Closed	—	—	16,968,166 5 10	—
	Total Consolidated Fund Loans,	12,328	687,021 15 6	35,174,162 14 0	449,854 19 6
	II. Loans out of Irish Church Fund, per Acts 32 Vic., c. 4, and 43 & 44 Vic., c. 141:—				
1	Improvement of Lands,	4,877	—	929,619 17 3	87,477 2 9
2	Sanitary Works,	78	—	80,384 18 0	1,890 6 1
3	National Works,	197	—	471,195 10 10	17,661 17 9
4	Relief of Distress,	7	—	11,983 12 4	909 6 4
5	Relief of Distress Grants,	—	—	16,000 5 0	—
6	Arterial Drainage,	21	—	9,184 1 0	60 19 11
	Total Church Fund Loans,	5,197	—	1,516,928 15 7	47,707 5 8
	Grand Total,	21,375	687,021 19 6	37,444,116 9 7	818,543 4 11

Advances and Repayments in the Year, the Total Advances and Repayments to the 31st March, 1889, the the Balances Outstanding.

I.—PUBLIC WORKS LOANS.

During the year ended 31st March, 1889, we have, with the approval of the Lords Commissioners of Her Majesty's Treasury, made 1,153 loans, amounting to £564,850, as compared with 1,321 loans for £829,766 in the year to 31st March, 1888, showing a decrease in number of 168 loans, and in money of £264,916, which is entirely due to the diminished sanctions under the Labourers Acts.

The following statement shows the twenty different purposes to which the loans sanctioned in the year, amounting to £564,850, have been allocated.

No of Loans.	LOANS SANCTIONED 1888-9.	Amount.
		£
2	Grand Juries of Counties,	1,997
3	Local Boards,	13,550
1	Inland Navigation,	2,000
1	Railways,	9,000
1	Reclamation of Waste Lands,	1,500
26	Labourers' Dwellings in Towns,	53,753
52	Glebe Loans,	10,989
46	Public Health Acts,	150,384
4	River Drainage, 26 & 27 Vic., c. 88,	4,970
1	Maintenance of Drainage Works,	20
1	Repairs of Post Roads,	1,000
1	Land Improvement—Preliminary Expenses,	2,000
7	Lunatic Asylums Buildings,	26,900
428*	Labourers Acts,	185,742
106	Land Improvement—Loans to Landlords,	30,125
59	National School Teachers' Residences,	13,154
10	Dispensary Houses,	6,900
8	Non-Vested Schools and Training Colleges,	5,430
2	Land Law Act, 1881, Sec. 19, Labourers' Cottages,	250
394	Do. Sec. 31, Loans to Tenants for Land Improvement.	37,060
1,153		£564,850

* No. of Electoral Divisions.

The above abstract contains only two loans which seem to require special notice :— (1.) An advance of £13,000 to the Irish Society, for the purpose of erecting a Town Hall at Londonderry. This loan, which is secured by a mortgage on a portion of the Society's estates in the county of Londonderry, is to be repaid by instalments over a period of twenty-five years, with interest at 4 per cent. (2.) An advance of £9,000 to the West Donegal Railway Company, forming part of a total capital of £19,000, which they are authorised to issue on the security of a Presentment made by the County Donegal, in pursuance of the Tramways and Public Companies Act, 1883, to complete their line into the town of Donegal. The working of this line, which runs from Stranorlar to Druminin, a distance of fourteen miles, has not been satisfactory, and it is confidently hoped that when the completion—a distance of four miles—is made into Donegal Town, the legitimate traffic of this district, which is now diverted to other channels, will be so increased as to enable the Company at least to meet the payments of interest on its loan capital of £40,000, a sum which we advanced in the year 1880, and the interest of which the earnings of the undertaking have hitherto been insufficient to discharge.

The other loans in the statement can be best referred to under their respective classes, as in our former reports.

The first in the list is the Housing of the Working Classes Act, 1885, which Act would have expired on the 31st December, 1888, but for its continuance for a further period of three years, ending 31st December, 1891, by the Public Works Loans Act, 1888. This Act enlarges the powers of the Labourers' Dwellings in Towns Act, 1866, by extending the term of repayment, where local bodies are concerned, from forty to fifty years, and by reducing the uniform rate of 4 per cent interest to a scale graduating from 3½ per cent. per annum for twenty years, to 3½ per cent. for fifty years. Under these favourable terms twenty-six loans have been sanctioned for £53,753, as compared with twenty loans for £34,747 in 1887–8. This brings the total authorized under these favourable conditions, during the four years since the Act passed, up to £218,416, or to an average of £54,604 per annum. Although this shows a considerable advance over the proceedings under the original Act of 1866, with its higher rate of interest, under which during nineteen years the total loans only amounted to £189,861, it still remains apparent that comparatively small use has been made of the liberal terms granted by the Act of 1885, with a view to the much needed requirement of improving the dwellings of the labouring poor residing in towns. The outlay under both Acts, amounting to £408,200, will probably when fully completed add upwards of 5,500 houses, and provide housing for 33,000 people.

The Glebe Loans Act of 1870 which, under various renewals, still continues its operations, shows a total advance of £421,620 to 991 borrowers on account of loans amounting to £427,599, which have been taken up by clergymen of the following religious denominations :—

		£
256	Irish Church,	122,137
487	Roman Catholic Church,	225,969
195	Presbyterian Church,	61,786
53	Wesleyan and other Churches,	17,707
991		£427,599

During the past year 52 loans have been sanctioned for new glebe houses, or additions thereto, for the total sum of £15,985.

Under the Public Health Acts 46 loans for £150,384 have been authorised, as compared with 35 loans, amounting to £64,778, in the previous year. These loans are in course of being applied to the following improvements :—

No.	—	—
		£
20	Water Works,	65,812
7	Sewerage Works,	4,687
3	Markets,	65,150
4	Flagging, &c.,	6,635
3	People's Parks,	5,100
4	Burial Grounds,	1,100
3	New Streets,	1,960
1	Baths, &c.,	1,500
1	Gas Works,	240
46		£150,384

The total authorizations in respect of which issues have been made for these and other sanitary works now amount to £1,615,914, on account of which we have advanced to 31st March, 1889, £1,521,911, including £74,472 issued during the year.

This total authorised sum has been granted for works of which the following is an abstract :—

	£
Sewerage,	809,860
Water Works,	791,814
Streets (Paving, &c.),	370,209
Public Baths,	18,150
Scavenging,	28,315
Buildings, Cemeteries, &c.,	106,866
	£1,615,914

The sanctions for arterial drainage works for the year are confined to 2 loans to the Killard and Ballycolliton Districts, for £1,026 and £1,424 respectively, and 2 supplemental loans for £2,520, to complete works commenced, making in all £4,970. This clearly points to an early cessation of such works, and to the fact that until some legislation is promoted which recognises the altered position between owners and occupiers of land, and which will throw the responsibility on those who are directly benefited, no

B

material progress in river drainage can be looked for. This principle is recognised in the three River Bills which were brought before the House last Session, and lately re introduced, as also in the Suck Drainage Bill.

Our efforts in the last year have been directed to such works as remained unfinished, with a view to their early completion. We have made Final Awards for the Districts of :—

> Ballyteigue and Kilmore, Follistown, Morning Star, Upper Nanny River, Nanny River, Upper, Owenroe,

and brought the sums advanced, together with interest accrued during progress of works, amounting to £43,373, under repayment, making in all £572,880, now under rentcharge.

The works in the Lough Erne District, on which a sum of £162,060 has been advanced, and those of the Suck Drainage, amounting to £88,786, are still incomplete. Should the Government Bill for the latter, now before Parliament, pass, the works should be completed in about three years.

The advances in the year under this head amount to £31,605, making a total of £785,202, including £6,136 out of the Church Fund, issued under the Act 26 & 27 Vic., cap. 88, which, with a further advance of £2,390,612, including £141,073 free grant, and £167,487 advanced by the public on debentures under the Act 5 & 6 Vic., cap. 89, gives a total expenditure for arterial drainage works of £3,175,814.

The operation for the improvement of land by owners in pursuance of the Land Improvement Act do not show any material change. One hundred and five loans for £30,125 have been authorized in the year, against 144 for £39,305 in 1887-8. This falling off of which has been continuous since the year 1884, when the sum of £126,235 was appropriated to these purposes, corroborates our former views that landlords will in future only improve lands which are in their own occupation. The number of owners is being · gradually increased by the Land Purchase Act, but a transfer of land on a very large scale could alone restore the former progress in land improvement.

The total advances made under this Act to 31st March, 1889, amount to £4,875,348.

We now beg to refer to the proceedings under the 31st section of the Land Law (Ireland) Act, 1881, which authorizes us to make advances to tenants for improvements on the security of their holdings, and to report that the position of these loans has not undergone any material change since last year. During the year 394 loans for £37,060 have been authorized, as compared with 444 loans for £36,575 in the previous year. The whole record of these loans is detailed in the following table :—

—	No. of Loans.	Amount.
		£
1882-83,	575	79,525
1883-84,	1,437	280,955
1884-85,	2,150	171,302
1885-86,	1,434	107,440
1886-87,	736	60,955
1887-88,	444	36,575
1888-89,	394	37,060
Total.	9,170	774,032

It would therefore appear that whatever causes have been influencing this class of borrowers, since 1884 when the applications began to diminish, not to avail themselves of this provision to a larger extent, are still in full operation. We were inclined to attribute this, to a great extent, to the enforcement of the regulation, that no loan could be considered or any subsequent advance made without the production of the receipt for the rent, and probably to this may be added the strict control which is exercised over the expenditure of each instalment of the loan before a further one is advanced.

Out of the sum of £774,032 authorized to be lent we have advanced £646,656 to the 31st March last, including £33,541 in the year.

The amount sanctioned in the year under the Labourers (Ireland) Acts, 1883 and 1885, in respect of 428 electoral divisions was £188,742, as compared with £463,261 to 497 electoral divisions in the year 1887-8. Out of the 161 Poor Law Unions of

Ireland 88 Unions, or more than one half, have availed themselves of the powers granted by these Acts, and have obtained loans in the aggregate to the amount of £1,009,740.

This sum has been taken up in the four provinces in the following proportions :—

						£
Munster,	.	.	45 Unions,	.	.	515,626
Leinster,	.	.	47 "	.	.	583,637
Connaught,	.	.	7 "	.	.	6,904
Ulster,	.	.	3 "	.	.	3,583
			88			£1,009,740

The expenditure of this amount has been proceeding rapidly. Up to 31st March, 1889, it amounted to £659,435, of which £242,597 was advanced within the year.

The Board make no doubt that the extraordinary divergence between the amounts required for meeting the purposes of this Act in Munster and Leinster, as compared with those in Connaught and Ulster, will attract your Lordships' attention ; but, as the Board merely make the advances under the instructions of the Local Government Board, they have not the requisite information to enable them to offer any explanation as to the causes which have led to these singular results of the legislation in question.

The other purposes to which loans have been granted do not require any special remarks. They include two loans to counties for £1,997 ; seven for the enlargement of Lunatic Asylums for £26,900 ; 59 for National School Teachers' residences for £18,164 ; 10 for Dispensary Houses for £6,900 ; and 8 for non-vested Schools and Training Colleges for £5,430.

CHURCH FUND LOANS.

The advances out of the £1,500,000 authorised to be made by the Relief of Distress Acts of 1880, out of the Irish Church Funds, amount to £1,269,933. The principal repayments in the year amounted to £47,707, and the interest payments to £10,728. The total repayments to 31st March, 1889, amount to £259,666 principal, and £64,185 in respect of interest.

The principal cancelled by redemptions by allowing borrowers 3 per cent. on moneys paid in anticipation, now amounts to £2,562.

ADVANCES AND REPAYMENTS.

The advances to Borrowers in the year out of moneys issued by the National Debt Commissioners were £557,022, as compared with £715,417 in 1887–88.

The total of all loan advances since the year 1817, to 31st March, 1889, amounts to £37,444,115.

The classified abstract at pages 6 and 7, shows how this large amount has been disposed of by repayments, remissions, and balances outstanding, viz. :—

					£
Total Repayments,	.	.	.	.	20,851,271
Total Remissions,	.	.	.	.	7,975,215
Written off from Local Loan Fund,	.	.	.	57,131
Total outstanding Balances,	.	.	.	8,560,498
					£37,444,115

This outstanding balance is represented, in the books of the office, by 21,313 open accounts, which are generally in course of repayment by half-yearly instalments.

The amounts received in the year were £516,562 in repayment of principal, and £252,987 in respect of interest, making together £769,549. Of this latter amount £711,113 was paid to the National Debt Commissioners, and £58,436 to the Irish Land Commission.

The repayments in the year, namely, £769,549, exceeded those of the year preceding, when they amounted to £538,021, by £231,528.

This large increase is accounted for by the redemption of the loans made to the Rathmines Town Commissioners, amounting to £119,000, to the repayment of principal due by Railway Companies £59,000, and some large redemptions on the Land Improvement Service, and the residue to the extension of the Loan Service.

The arrears of principal and interest (due and not paid) which on the 31st March, 1887, were £432,586, and in March, 1888, £426,017, now amount to £435,336.

B 2

The following Abstract shows the services on which these arrears occur :—

COMPARATIVE RETURN OF LOAN ARREARS.

—	31 March, 1887.	31 March, 1888.	31 March, 1889.
	£	£	£
Public Works Loans generally, . . .	6,517	14,782	21,773
Clare Slob Reclamation Loan, . .	11,113	17,412	23,292
Public Health Act, ...	5,769	9,997	7,333
Railways, ...	269,350	249,338	369,918
Land Charges, ...	88,289	95,533	90,136
Seed Supply, ...	41,968	34,967	33,886
Bad and Doubtful Debts, . . .	56,889	—	—
	432,586	420,019	436,388

It will be seen from the foregoing statement that the gross arrears have increased during the year by a sum of £9,317, but this is more than accounted for by the growth of arrears on Railway loans amounting to £20,580. The arrears on Public Works Loans, £21,773, arise on Harbour Loans, Labourers' Dwellings, Glebe Loans, Labourers Act, &c., but in the main on Harbour loans, which are in arrear to the extent of £17,335. A large portion of it is due to the necessary delay in getting Presentments from the guaranteeing counties, and £6,195 is due on Galway Harbour, the repayments of which have fallen into arrear from the necessity of renewing the Dock Gates, and a further sum of £3,705, arises on the Wicklow Harbour loan handed over to us by the Public Works Loans Commissioners, England. The Clare Slob Reclamation Loan also shows an increase of £5,880, being the amount of interest accrued during the year, which must go on until this undertaking is disposed of. The Public Health Loans, although considerably increased in amount and extent, show a decrease in the arrears on the former year of £2,664. The Land Charges arrears have undergone some sensible reduction, notwithstanding the special difficulties which occurred in recovering moneys from the owners of land in many parts of the country. The Seed Supply Loans arrears have likewise been reduced.

The following Table shows the arrears on Land Charges in each of the ten years ending with March, 1889 :—

	£			£
31st March, 1880, . .	13,349	31st March, 1885, . .		54,173
„ 1881, . .	23,625	„ 1886, . .		77,967
„ 1882, . .	41,475	„ 1887, . .		88,289
„ 1883, . .	54,636	„ 1888, . .		95,533
„ 1884, . .	54,104	„ 1889, . .		90,136

The Railway Loan arrears continue to advance ; at the close of last year they stood at £249,888, comprising £151,291 and £98,047, for principal and interest respectively ; they now amount to £269,918, of which £156,968 are due for principal, and £112,950 for interest. It is obvious where the earnings of railway lines do not afford sufficient surpluses to discharge the interest, on account of which £112,950 is now in arrear, that it is quite impossible for such Companies to raise on their debenture capitals amounts to discharge the principal debts. As affording, however, the best proof of growing prosperity it is satisfactory to note that during the last year two Companies (the Ballymena and Larne Railway and the Ilen Valley Railway) have not only paid off their principal instalments in arrear, but have been able to discharge their principal debts in advance of their becoming due, and we can only hope that some other lines will soon be able to adopt the same course.

OUTSTANDING BALANCES.

The outstanding balances which at the end of March, 1888, amounted to £8,578,565, have by the operations of the year just ended decreased to £8,560,499.

The following statement shows the rates of interest chargeable on the several amounts, making the aggregate balances in each year ended 31st March, 1887, 1888, and 1889, respectively:—

—	31 March, 1887.	31 March, 1888.	31 March, 1889.
	£	£	£
Free of Interest,	98,386	83,847	54,493
3 per cent.,	6,000	6,000	6,000
3¼ „	34,341	404,508	423,009
3½ „	288,576	308,964	387,029
3¾ „	36,334	56,108	61,440
3⅞ „	3,978,311	3,483,485	3,530,438
3 „	306,676	433,894	537,636
4 „	1,178,910	1,907,632	1,810,043
4½ „	358,198	356,001	349,604
5 „	225,668	233,774	108,514
Advances on which interest is deferred, pending the completion of the works,	229,268	266,549	263,684
Total Local Loans Fund,	7,081,581	7,540,827	7,571,868
Church Fund Loans -- at 1 per cent.,	1,382,018	1,037,738	988,636
	8,163,579	8,578,565	*8,540,499

* Exclusive of £57,131 written off from the Account of the Assets of the Local Loans Fund.

The average rate chargeable on the advances out of the Local Loans Fund was £3 13s. 3d., on the 31st March, 1887; £3 13s. 4d., on the 31st March, 1888; and £3 13s. 3d., on the 31st March, 1889, but the interest realised in the year did not average more than £3 6s. 10d. per cent. on the principal sum outstanding on the 1st April, 1888.

Estimate for Loans.

We have submitted in the ordinary way our estimate of the probable requirements for the year 1889-90, on account of which £1,000,000 will, it is considered, he sufficient to discharge all possible demands.

Labouring Classes' Lodging and Dwellings Acts.

29 & 80 Vic., c. 44, 1866, and the Housing of the Working Classes Act, 1885, 48 & 49 Vic., c. 72.

Since the passing of the first Act above referred to, in 1866, to the close of the year 1884-85, a period of nineteen years, loans were made under the provisions of that and the amending Acts, amounting to £281,334, for the erection of dwellings for 3,316 families, the rate of interest charged being 4 per cent.

The more favourable terms granted by your Lordships' minute of 23rd January, 1886, as to the rate of interest on such Loans has had the effect of stimulating in some degree those desirous of providing improved dwellings for the labouring classes, and it will be observed that during the year 1887-88 twenty Loans were made to the amount of £34,746 10s. for building 397 dwellings, while during the past year applications have been received for Loans amounting to £78,469 for building labourers' dwellings, of which twenty-six, to the amount of £53,752 10s., have been sanctioned for 575 dwellings.

The following abstract, No. 1, shows the number and amount of the Loans made each year during the periods referred to, and abstract No. 2 gives the particulars as to locality, &c., of the Loans made within the past year.

ABSTRACT No. 1.

Year.	No. of applications sanctioned.	Amount sanctioned.	No. of families to be accommodated.
		£ s.	
1866–67,	Nil }	658 0	{ Nil
1867–68,	1 }		8
1888–69,	Nil	—	Nil
1869–70,	1	500 0	10
1870–71,	1	4,146 0	125
1871–79,	2	1,050 0	46
1872–73,	3	7,175 0	108
1873–74,	7	12,250 0	261
1874–75,	1	910 0	15
1875–76,	7	24,242 0	259
1876–77,	8	11,100 0	131
1877–78,	8	23,614 0	272
1878–79,	10	7,100 0	81
1879–80,	19	31,858 0	351
1880–81,	17	28,870 0	302
1881–82,	17	33,674 0	453
1882–83,	16	21,187 0	270
1883–84,	16	40,052 0	397
1884–85,	12	22,360 0	328
1885–86,	20	50,755 0	713
1886–87,	34	79,161 0	852
1887–88,	20	24,746 10	397
1888–89,	26	53,752 10	575
Total,	234	466,499 0	5,953

ABSTRACT No. II.

Locality.	Number of Dwellings to be built.	Amount of loan sanctioned.
		£
Ballinasloe,	8	400
Belfast,	50	2,680
Cork,	70	4,197
Dublin,	333	33,628
Enniskillen,	28	8,097
Galway,	13	870
Irvinestown,	4	200
Lecan,	10	1,100
Milford, co. Armagh,	30	4,500
Omagh,	4	380
Sligo,	3	160
Wexford,	26	2,500
Total,	575	53,752

To secure that the loans sanctioned shall be applied to the erection of such dwellings as come fairly within the scope of the Acts, and are in every respect suitable to the means and requirements of the labouring classes, it is made a condition with the borrower that the rents to be charged are not to exceed certain specified sums, such rents being fixed on consideration of the locality and the class of labourers for whom accommodation is required. This arrangement has had the effect of limiting the cost of the erection of dwellings built under the loans referred to, and thus securing, as far as practicable, their being permanently available for occupation by the labouring classes.

GLEBE LOANS.

33 & 34 Vic., c. 112; 34 & 35 Vic., c. 100; 38 & 39 Vic., c. 80; 41 Vic., c. 6;
43 & 44 Vic., c. 2; 49 Vic., c. 6.

Fifty-seven applications for loans have been received during the year, amounting to £17,237, and 53 loans have been granted for £15,985. The issues for the year have amounted to £11,039 6s. 8d. Since passing of the first Act, 1870, we have received 1,306 applications, of which the following is an abstract of those on which issues were made to 31st March, 1889.

—	Amount.	No.
	£	
Church of Ireland, . . .	122,137	256
Roman Catholic, . . .	226,969	457
Presbyterian, . . .	61,786	125
Wesleyan and other, . . .	17,707	53
	427,599	991

NATIONAL SCHOOL TEACHERS' RESIDENCES (IRELAND) ACTS.

38 & 39 Vic., c. 82; 42 & 43 Vic., c. 74.

Seventy-three applications under these Acts have been received during the year for loans, amounting to £16,295, and 59, amounting to £13,163 10s. have been granted. Some are still under consideration. The amount issued on this service during the year has been £12,453 10s., and from the passing of the Acts, £87,711 10s.

DISPENSARY HOUSES (IRELAND) ACT.

42 & 43 Vic., c. 25.

The applications under this Act have been 101, amounting to £67,651.
Of these sixteen were received during the year ending 31st March, 1889, for £11,034. The total amount issued has been £56,951, of which £6,788 was paid out during the present year.

LOANS FOR SCHOOLS AND TRAINING COLLEGES (IRELAND) ACT, 1884.

47 & 48 Vic., cap. 22.

Under the provisions of the above Act, which was passed in 1884, the Commissioners of Public Works may, on the recommendation of the Commissioners of National Education and with the approval of the Lords Commissioners of Her Majesty's Treasury, on being satisfied as to the sufficiency of the security, make loans for the purpose of assisting any person in the erection, enlargement, structural improvement, or purchase of a house to be used as a non-vested National school or training college, or in the improvement of any existing non-vested National school or training college, or in the acquisition or improvement of a farm not exceeding twenty-five acres in extent connected with a non-vested National school or training college, to be used for the purpose of agricultural instruction, or for the purpose of discharging any debt due and incurred before the 19th day of May, 1884, in the erection, enlargement, structural improvement, or purchase of a house to be used as a training college, and loans made for any of the foregoing purposes are repayable by an annual rentcharge of five per cent. in thirty-five years. The provisions of the Act have not been availed of to the extent anticipated, only thirteen applications having been received during the past year for loans amounting to £4,965.

PUBLIC LIBRARIES ACTS. (40 & 41 Vic., cc. 15 & 54.)

No application has been received for an advance under these Acts.

INDUSTRIAL SCHOOLS (IRELAND) ACT, 1885. (48 Vic., c. 19.)

An application has been received from the Co. Cork Grand Jury for an advance of £500, under this Act, to alter and enlarge the Marble Hill Industrial School, Blackrock, Co. Cork.

REFORMATORY INSTITUTIONS (IRELAND) ACT, 1881.

No application has been received for an advance under this Act.

LAND IMPROVEMENT.

Under this head we commence by giving, as usual, the numbers of applications for loans, and the amounts issued in each year from the commencement, in the year 1847, to the end of the financial year, 31st March, 1889 :—

—	No. of Applications.	Amount Issued.	—	No. of Applications.	Amount Issued.
1847, June to Dec. (inclusive),	1,254	£72,790	1869-70, . . .	166	£83,778
1848, . . .	571	386,160	1870-71, .	159	77,960
1849, . . .	643	378,536	1871-72, .	160	83,585
1850, . . .	636	260,334	1872-73, .	333	76,290
1851, . . .	340	145,653	1873-74, .	224	99,572
1852, . . .	164	86,542	1874-75, .	245	102,006
1853, . . .	154	55,454	1875-76, .	365	96,730
1854, . . .	123	49,293	1876-77, .	218	121,405
1855, . . .	96	35,180	1877-78, .	278	121,345
1856, . . .	108	32,510	1878-79, .	319	125,370
1857, . . .	114	31,574	1879-80, { Relief, 2,144 Ordinary, 463 }	2,607	e 234,810
1858, . . .	112	35,534			
1859, . . .	111	29,334	1880-81, .	638	e 766,659
1860, . . .	135	36,902	1881-82, .	401	a 298,583
1861, . . .	154	36,656	1882-83, .	451	a 138,536
1862, . . .	184	61,375	1883-84, .	503	a 123,082
1863, . . .	138	68,830	1884-85, .	395	a 117,420
1864, . . .	132	58,430	1885-86, .	293	ab 79,578
1865, . . .	90	46,215	1886-87, .	219	ab 59,192
1866, . . .	98	36,296	1887-88, .	181	b 48,752
1867, . . .	145	39,180	1888-89, .	148	b 31,793
1868-9, . . .	179	84,973			

Having many opportunities of learning the causes which work to prevent a larger number of loans being obtained, we are confirmed in the belief, stated in our report of last year, that the main deterring cause is the unsettled state of the relations between landlords and tenants. Landowners will not now apply for loans in respect of lands in the hands of their tenants, while, as regards the improvement of land in their own hands, they are in many cases stopped from obtaining advances by our requirement that arrears of rent-charges on former loans must be paid up before new applications are entertained.

The loans under which works have been commenced within the past year are classified under the following heads :—

Class of Work	No. of Loans	Amount Sanctioned.	Average of each Loan.
		£	£
Drainage and other Land Works, . .	35	8,540	244
Farm Buildings, . . .	63	15,970	253
Labourers' Cottages, . . .	13	2,225	171
Mixed Loans—including Buildings and Land Works, . . .	15	3,440	230
Totals, . . .	126	30,175	—
General Average per Loan, .	—	—	239

a Includes issues under Relief of Distress Act.   b Includes issues under Section 19, Land Law Act.

There were 148 applications for loans during the past financial year, and of these 86 have been sanctioned; but 19 loans previously applied for were also approved within that time, making a total of 105 amounting to £30,125. There were therefore 62 which did not arrive at the stage of sanction for the following reasons :—

Cause of Delay or Rejection.	No. of Cases.
Failed to show Title,	9
Stopped owing to default in expending previous Loans, or in paying Rentcharge,	2
Transferred to Land Law Division,	6
Withdrawn,	5
Under consideration,	33
Refused,	7
Total number of Applications not come to maturity,	62

The following table gives the number of loans and the sums issued in the several counties in Ireland up to the 31st March, 1889 :—

SCHEDULE showing the NUMBER of LOANS and AMOUNTS ISSUED from commencement of Aor.

Name of County.	No. of Loans.	Amounts Issued.			Total No. of Loans.	Total Amount Issued.		
		£	s.	d.		£	s.	d.
NORTHERN DIVISION.								
Antrim,	195	121,593	0	0				
Londonderry,	161	66,728	0	0				
Donegal,	287	185,571	0	0				
Fermanagh,	156	81,100	0	0				
Tyrone,	230	148,905	0	0				
Armagh,	65	21,623	0	0				
Down,	138	92,459	0	0	1,292	725,579	0	0
MIDLAND AND EASTERN.								
Cavan,	150	53,270	0	0				
Monaghan,	94	43,956	0	0				
Longford,	315	177,601	0	0				
Louth,	83	36,634	0	0				
Meath,	387	191,230	0	0				
Westmeath,	360	93,290	0	0				
Dublin,	236	81,662	0	0				
Kildare,	267	133,962	0	0				
King's,	199	59,963	0	0				
Queen's,	311	149,467	0	0				
Wicklow,	325	118,596	0	0				
Carlow,	206	105,064	0	0				
Kilkenny,	172	64,763	0	0				
Wexford,	277	131,091	0	0	3,216	1,451,179	0	0
WESTERN.								
Sligo,	284	134,577	0	0				
Leitrim,	196	74,235	0	0				
Mayo,	483	225,769	0	0				
Roscommon,	454	225,998	0	0				
Galway,	756	378,648	0	0				
Clare,	452	165,688	0	0	2,625	1,205,235	0	0
SOUTHERN.								
Limerick,	749	370,531	0	0				
Tipperary,	534	193,447	0	0				
Waterford,	151	66,100	0	0				
Cork,	1,251	416,498	0	0				
Kerry,	713	463,769	0	0	3,398	1,515,385	0	0
Totals,					10,531	4,875,345	0	0

C

Main and Thorough Drainage.

The number of loans sanctioned for works, of which thorough drainage forms the principal part, since the commencement in 1847 to the 31st March in this year, is 8,065, for £3,678,597, and of this number 35 loans for £10,160 were approved during the year ending 31st March, 1889.

Planting for Shelter.

Since the passing of the Act 29 and 30 Vic., c. 40, 103 loans for £22,420 have been made, and of that number, 2, for £950, were sanctioned during the year now reported on.

Farm Buildings.

For this class of work 2,420 loans have been sanctioned since the passing of the Act 13 & 14 Vic., c. 19, the amount being £1,063,590. This includes 55 loans, for £15,995, approved during the past financial year.

Dwellings for Agricultural Labourers.

The number of loans granted for this class of work since the passing of the Act 28 Vic., c. 19, is 664, for £325,660 ; of this number 13, for £3,020, were approved since our last Report.

Land Law (Ireland) Act, 1881.—Loans to Tenants.

Sections 19 and 31.

The above quoted Sections are those under which the Board have power to advance money for improvement of tenants' holdings. Under the former the total number of loans sanctioned up to the 31st March, 1888, is 248, for £14,351, and of this total instalments amounting to £12,841 have been issued to borrowers, who, pursuant to the orders of the Land Commission, have proceeded to erect dwellings for labourers on their farms. The total number of loans granted under Section 31 up to the 31st March, 1888, was 9,185, the amount issued being £646,656. Of this sum £33,541 was issued during the past financial year. The number of applications for loans lodged during the year 1888–9 was 613, which shows a decrease of 50 as compared with the previous year.

The reports of some of our most experienced Inspectors show that the still unsettled state of the country operates to prevent schemes of improvement being undertaken, and causes a falling off in the number of loans applied for. As rent takes precedence of the Board's loan arrears are a barrier to the tenant obtaining a loan, and it is one of the Board's requirements that before he obtains an issue of money he must show that his rent is not twelve months in arrear. It is satisfactory to note an improvement in the status of the borrowers obtaining loans under this Section, and an increase in the average amount of loan. While the average in 1884–5 was as low as £75, it has now risen to £105. We continue to receive information from our local officers as to the beneficial results of the expenditure of these advances. The Inspectors concur in the opinion that the acquisition of their holdings by the tenants under the Land Purchase Act would give a stimulus to loan operations. In the Appendix (B) will be found extracts from the reports of the Local Inspectors.

Hay Barns are considered in this uncertain climate a necessary erection for successful farming, and for many years we have assisted farmers by means of loans for the construction of this essential feature of the modern farmsteading, but it is only within the past few years that occupiers have to any appreciable extent availed themselves of this assistance. It is, now, however, satisfactory to observe that during the past year applications for this class of structure have largely increased, thus affording proof that the occupiers of medium-sized farms have at length realised that it is only by the improved methods which constitute what is termed modern farming that they can hope successfully to contend with adverse seasons and foreign competition. From the number of applications received during the past two months, the desire to erect hay barns appears to be increasing. This shows that the past operations of the Board have resulted in calling the attention of farmers to improved methods, and in creating a desire on their part to avail themselves of these resources in the cultivation of their holdings.

The importance of this subject is evident from the Agricultural Returns, which state that at the low rate of £2 5s. per ton the Irish hay crop is worth on an average £9,000,000 per annum. Some estimates would show that a hay barn will in an average season effect a saving of 10 per cent. on the value of the crop; but allowing that even 5 per cent. is saved, it would represent an increase of £450,000 per annum in the value of this important crop if the use of hay barns was universal throughout the country.

The following table gives the distribution by Counties of the sums issued for all classes of work under the 31st Section of the Land Law (Ireland) Act, 1881:—

SCHEDULE showing the NUMBER of LOANS SANCTIONED and AMOUNTS ISSUED up to the 31st MARCH, 1889.

PROVINCE AND COUNTY	Number of Loans Sanctioned.			Amounts Sanctioned.			Total Sums.		
	To 31st Mar., 1888.	Year ending 31st Mar., 1889.	Total Number.	To 31st Mar., 1888.	Year ending 31st Mar., 1889.	Total Sanctioned.	To 31st Mar., 1888.	Year ending 31st Mar., 1889.	Total Issued.
				£	£	£	£	£	£
LEINSTER:									
Carlow,	47	2	49	6,745	310	7,055	4,331	177	4,508
Dublin,	48	6	54	7,785	800	8,585	6,236	1,027	7,263
Kildare,	94	10	104	15,340	1,330	16,670	11,963	543	12,526
Kilkenny,	78	10	88	7,660	1,440	9,100	5,802	710	6,512
King's,	160	7	167	14,310	745	15,055	11,521	623	12,144
Longford,	247	7	254	21,585	825	22,410	18,487	977	19,464
Louth,	27	3	30	3,890	190	4,080	3,392	182	3,474
Meath,	80	11	91	15,005	1,045	16,050	12,612	891	13,503
Queen's,	64	6	70	6,755	565	7,320	5,060	577	5,537
Westmeath,	183	13	196	19,865	1,875	21,740	15,747	798	16,545
Wexford,	69	9	78	7,230	700	7,930	5,970	610	6,580
Wicklow,	61	10	71	7,100	1,015	8,115	5,421	1,242	6,603
Totals,	1,156	95	1,251	132,270	10,540	144,110	106,462	8,366	114,828
MUNSTER:									
Clare,	586	14	600	48,155	1,250	49,405	40,822	1,662	42,484
Cork,	1,512	63	1,575	128,130	5,410	133,540	109,593	6,410	116,003
Kerry,	805	21	826	46,805	1,915	48,720	36,336	1,552	37,888
Limerick,	415	29	444	40,120	3,485	43,605	32,384	2,396	34,752
Tipperary,	290	82	322	27,900	2,625	30,525	22,177	2,628	24,805
Waterford,	39	6	45	4,900	420	5,320	3,195	568	3,783
Totals,	3,647	165	3,812	296,010	15,105	311,115	244,467	15,228	259,895
ULSTER:									
Antrim,	63	10	73	6,775	840	7,615	5,828	817	6,645
Armagh,	70	4	74	4,530	295	4,825	3,584	363	3,947
Cavan,	561	22	583	37,650	1,625	39,275	31,757	1,276	33,033
Donegal,	309	7	316	15,262	495	15,757	3,958	844	4,802
Down,	43	3	46	4,415	300	4,715	12,938	472	13,410
Fermanagh,	114	5	119	7,970	360	8,330	6,303	237	6,440
Londonderry,	85	7	92	6,300	670	6,970	5,304	532	5,836
Monaghan,	59	2	61	4,665	100	4,765	2,597	100	2,787
Tyrone,	200	5	205	15,950	305	16,255	12,312	403	12,715
Totals,	1,403	65	1,468	103,517	4,890	108,407	84,481	5,134	89,615
CONNAUGHT:									
Galway,	521	15	536	42,625	1,220	43,845	36,657	1,273	37,930
Leitrim,	549	12	561	34,785	860	35,645	30,966	660	31,636
Mayo,	916	13	929	67,565	1,220	68,785	58,755	966	59,731
Roscommon,	393	16	409	29,475	1,330	30,805	24,444	1,124	25,568
Sligo,	405	14	419	30,570	1,685	32,255	26,853	810	27,663
Totals,	2,784	70	2,854	204,830	6,315	211,135	177,705	4,813	182,518
Grand Totals,	8,790	395	9,185	737,517	37,150	774,767	613,115	33,541	646,656

We also beg to submit a statement classifying the loans in which works have been completed under the different descriptions of work, to the 31st March, 1889 :—

Description of Work.	Amounts Expended		
	From passing of Act to 31st March, 1888.	For year ending 31st March, 1889.	Total from passing of Act to 31st March, 1889.
	£ s. d.	£ s. d.	£ s. d.
Drainage, Fencing, Farm Roads, and other Land Works,	291,014 8 6	38,606 14 6	329,621 3 0
Farm Houses and Offices,	235,587 1 3	26,782 4 4	262,369 5 7
Labourers' Cottages, 19th section,	9,091 10 10	145 0 0	9,936 10 10
Labourers' Cottages, 31st section,	6,480 16 2	1,097 2 5	7,577 18 7
Scutch Mills for Flax,	262 17 3	55 5 0	318 2 3
	542,436 14 0	66,686 6 3	609,123 0 3

The number of loans in which the amounts sanctioned have been expended, and the works certified as completed is 7,209, and those in which the works were still in progress on the 31st March, 1889, were 1,173.

II.—VOTED SERVICES.

Under this second head of our duties, comprising those services which are created by, or maintained from, annual votes of Parliament, the accounts detailed in the Appendix (A) record the following expenditures on each to 31st March, 1889, and the second column shows the expenditure on the same votes for the preceding year 1887-88.

	1888-89.	1887-88.
Class I.	£	£
Public Buildings, Ireland,	184,725	204,378
Royal University, Ireland,	130	2,319
Science and Art Buildings, Dublin,	39,158	41,979
Class II.		
Public Works Office,	40,482	46,014
	264,495	294,690

Showing the total charge against the Consolidated Fund for the year to be £264,495. But as from these services we have derived rents, tolls, fees, &c., amounting to £10,403, of which the sum of £10,233 has been paid or will be paid over to Her Majesty's Exchequer in aid of Revenue—the net charge amounts to £254,262.

PUBLIC BUILDINGS.

General Observations.

The several buildings in the Board's charge have been carefully attended to as regards their repair and maintenance, the execution of such minor alterations and improvements as the services required, together with the supply and maintenance of the necessary furniture and fittings, and the several articles required for cleaning, fuel, and light.

The Board have to report that the following new works and important alterations have been carried out during the year :—

Coast Guard Stations.—The new station at Mulroy is very nearly completed, and considerable additions and improvements have been made to the old stations at Crookhaven, Annalong, Ballycotton, Ballyakelliga.

Royal Naval Reserve.—The new battery and drill shed at Upper Cove, Kinsale, is in a very forward state.

Ordnance Survey Office.—The quarters for unmarried soldiers have been finished, and are now occupied. These quarters, together with those built last year for the married soldiers, complete the additions to the Mountjoy Barrack. The work has been necessarily spread over two years, as the old buildings could only be given up in sections, as new accommodation became available.

General Survey and Valuation.—The works necessary to adapt the back premises (formerly coach-house and stabling, and much dilapidated) for the reception of office records, have been carried out.

R. I. Constabulary Buildings.—The shed for sheltering the brakes at the Depot, Phœnix Park, with harness room, etc., has been completed.

The new barrack at Boherbuoy (Collooney-street), Limerick, was commenced, and fair progress has been made, and the same is to be reported as to the first of the four District Head-quarters Barracks at Mount Pottinger-road, Belfast, but unfortunately the death of the contractor has caused the suspension of the work, but arrangements are being made for proceeding with it, and the Board fully expect that the building will be completed during the current financial year.

The works for the conversion of Roscommon Bridewell into a barrack have been completed, as also those for the improvement of the barrack at Dingle, and the fitting up as a barrack the premises acquired at Carlow, Youghal, Edenderry, and Athlone, and similar works at Great Victoria-street, and Henry-street, Belfast, are in a very forward state.

Dundrum Asylum.—The additional staircases necessary to secure the safe exit of the patients in the event of fire are completed.

Science and Art Buildings.—The new office for the Head Master at the Schools of Art, and stores for materials, pupils' work, &c., are completed.

National Education Buildings.—Grants towards the erection of new schools, and improvements of existing schools, to the amount of £41,495 2s. 8d., have been paid, as against £51,521 13s. 10d., in 1887-8, and arrangements have been made to restrict the expenditure under this head to the amount sanctioned for this service during the current year.

Only two grants have been made for teachers' residences, as more favourable conditions are offered, by way of loans, for the provision of such buildings.

Custom Offices.—The redistribution of the space in the Belfast Custom House, formerly occupied by the Postal and Telegraph Department, has been carried out, and now affords accommodation for a Branch Post office, Offices for the Local Marine Board, and Surveyors' Department of the Board of Trade, and improved offices for the District Registry, under the Court of Probate.

Postal and Telegraph Offices.—The new Post Office at Kilkenny, and the Telegraph Stores in Dublin, have been completed. The proposal to build a new office at Clonmel has been abandoned through failure to acquire the intended site. A contract has been entered into for the District Office, at Fairview, Dublin, but little has yet been done, as possession of the site has only been recently obtained.

DEPOSITORIES FOR PAROCHIAL RECORDS.

Act 39 & 40 Vic., c. 58.

Under the provisions of this Act, inspections of proposed Depositories have been made in 15 cases, and reports thereon forwarded to the Deputy Keeper of the Records.

PARKS AND GARDENS.

The Phœnix Park.—The several buildings, roads, plantations, &c., have been properly maintained, and the People's Garden continues to be highly appreciated by the public as a place of recreation.

St. Stephen's-green Park has been maintained in good order, and has had its attractions increased by the addition of a handsome band stand, as the Jubilee memorial of the members of the Dublin Metropolitan Police.

New Museum of Science and Art and National Library Buildings.

The erection of these buildings has been proceeded with in a very satisfactory manner, and with as much rapidity as the proper construction of the work admitted.

The Museum Building has been completed with the exception of the arrangements for lighting (not yet decided on) and of some finishing works in connection with the heating appliances, the flooring, and the stone carvings. Arrangements have been made for the supply of the necessary cases for the exhibits, a large portion of which it is anticipated will be delivered within the next three months.

The National Library Building, though not so advanced as the Museum, is also progressing satisfactorily. The structure of the building, with the exception of portion of the front colonade, has been completed, and the heating appliances and fittings for the Book Stores and Reading Rooms are in an advanced state.

A contract has been made for the entrance gates and enclosure railings to the court yard, and for the formation of the grounds to suit the levels of the new buildings, and this work is now in progress.

It is anticipated that both buildings, and the work in connection with the enclosure and formation of the court yard, will be completed early in the autumn.

Royal Harbours.

Kingstown, County Dublin.

The works at this Harbour have been kept in good order during the year. At the back of the West Pier a shed has been erected for the convenience of the Dunleary fishermen, and the approach to same improved. The accommodation for the Mail Steamers, on the eastern side of the Mail Packet Pier, has been extended by sub-marine blasting and dredging. Dredging has been also carried on inside of the Traders' Wharf. A quantity of 4,697 tons of silt has been dredged during the year.

The dredging of the remainder of the Harbour, which is not pressing, was suspended in the month of July, and the dredging staff, dredger, and barges removed to Howth Harbour where the deepening of the entrance was urgently demanded.

Water has been supplied to Her Majesty's ships, the vessels of the Irish Lights Board, yachts, and trading vessels, and a quantity of 742 tons of ballast supplied to the latter.

For a summary of Rainfall and Tidal Observations, as also numbers, &c., of vessels visiting the Harbour, see Appendix C.

Howth Harbour.—County Dublin.

The works have been maintained in good order during the year. It is satisfactory that the sea slope of the East Pier, which is the chief defence of the Harbour, has not required any repair.

Your Lordships having ordered that the entrance of the Harbour should be deepened, the necessary plant and materials were procured, partly from Kingstown Harbour, and by purchase where not on hands. This work was commenced in the month of August, and a quantity of 10,922 tons was removed, and deposited near the Railway Station, at the end of the financial year.

The number of boats engaged in fishing during the year was 900, viz.:—Scotch, 103 ; Irish, 74 ; Cornish, 17 ; and Manx, 6.

9,549 mease of herrings were sold at an average price of 18s. 9d. per mease.

Year.	Boats.	Mease—Herrings.	Average Price.
1884—1885	258	6,340	34s. 0d. per mease.
1885—1886	393	2,477	33s. 6d. „
1886—1887	317	9,492	17s. 4d. „
1887—1888	223	8,777	17s. 1d. „
1888—1889	900	9,549	18s. 9d. „

The imports consisted of 3,276 tons coal, 124 tons of salt, and 238 tons of bricks and tiles. The exports were 5,215 barrels of herrings, which exceeded those of the previous year by 985 barrels.

Dunmore Harbour.—County Waterford.

The works of this Harbour have been kept in good order during the year.   The toe of the sea slope, which has been the cause of much expense, was made good, and has not suffered by the gales of last winter.

Mr. Frederick George Kent, having made application for a site adjacent to the Harbour, for the purpose of erecting a fish curing establishment, it was submitted to His Excellency the Lord Lieutenant, under the provisions of the Act 58 Geo. III., cap. 72 ; the necessary sanction was obtained on the 25th March, 1888 ; and a lease containing the usual covenants was made to him at the yearly rent of £10 10s.

Within the past year 73 large cutters and 12 steam trawlers fished in the offing, of which 50 fished out of Dunmore ; the remainder, thirty-five, " iced," and brought their fish to the English markets.

The quantity of herrings sold here during last year was 14,485 mease ; and realized £10,020.   The lobster and long line fishermen did remarkably well ; lobsters averaged 9s. 3d., and crabs 2s. 2d. per dozen.

During the year there were over 1,000 tons of general cargo imported, and 90 exported.

The number of fishing boats employed was as follows :—English, 29 ; Scotch, 42 ; Welsh, 9 ; Manx, 49 ; and Irish, 174.

Donaghadee Harbour.—County Down.

The slope of the South Pier stood well during the past year, but the toe had to be strengthened, as opportunities offered, with heavy stones, and 1,180 square yards of sea pavement was rejointed with concrete.   The works generally have been kept in good order.

At Lennon's Wharf the old rubble wall, which was in a bad state, was taken down and rebuilt in concrete.   During such times, as the state of the weather prevented the labourers from working on the sea side of the piers, they were employed in removing some dangerous rocks within the Harbour.

The coal trade to this port is still improving a little, the imports of the year being about 429 tons over those of last year, but this is the only business carried on at present.   These were not exported during the past year, although the year before seventeen vessels left with 1,357 tons of native timber.   A few fishing boats called with herrings during the season, and sold to small dealers in Donaghadee about 239 mease at prices from 8s. 6d. to 17s. 6d. per mease.   Fifty-four fishing boats called here for shelter on their passage to and from the regular fishing ports.

During the year 44 cargo vessels (18,311 tons) and 54 fishing boats used the Harbour.

Ardglass Harbour.—County Down.

The sea slope of this Harbour of old construction, which is founded on a heap of *pierres perdus*, requires continual attention, as is the case wherever this mode of construction has been adopted at an insufficient depth.   The work has stood well during the winter, but some of this rubble stone has been carried round the head into the Harbour, and must be removed as opportunity offers.

The south end of the Harbour has been deepened next Ardglass Castle, and the accommodation of the Harbour thereby much improved.

The works have been preserved in good order.

The weather being unfavourable the herring fishing at this Harbour did not commence until 13th June, and from that time to 18th October, the total quantity brought into this Harbour only amounted to 11,380 mease ; the highest price obtained was 33s., and the lowest 8s.; the average all through the season was equal to 16s. per mease.   The fishing was very good during the fortnight ending 30th June ; the quantity taken during that time was 6,957 mease ; the remainder of the season was very bad, and taking it altogether, it was the worst season for many years past.

For about four weeks in June and July, from two to four steamers were in the Harbour daily looking for herrings to carry them to the English and Scotch markets, but the supply was so very small they had to remain for days waiting to get even a few boxes, and at last they left altogether about the 18th July, and the market for the remainder of the year was in the hands of small local buyers. During the past winter a few stray trawlers and one boat fishing from here landed about four tons of different kinds of fish (conger, skate, ling, plaice, &c.), and sold them at 6s. to 11s. per cwt.

The number of boats fishing from here last season amounted in all to 229, viz. :—

English	Scotch	Manx	Irish
1	87	40	101

During the year 22 cargo vessels (2,070 tons) used the Harbour.

In addition to the above, twenty-eight steam tugs called here during the year either for shelter or for orders.

SHANNON DRAINAGE WORKS.

The new channel at Lough Allen has been nearly all excavated, about 160,000 cubic yards having been done. The concrete work for the sluices and bridge is about half built, and the ironwork has arrived and will be soon erected. The excavation at Killaloe, on the Tipperary side of the river, has been nearly all taken out as far as the edge of the lake. There has been altogether about 78,000 cubic yards excavated, mostly rock. The navigation wall is partly built. The season was unfavourable for work in the bed of the river at Killaloe, as the sluices had to be kept open most of the time, in consequence of which the dredging above the weir could not be proceeded with.

INLAND NAVIGATIONS.

ULSTER CANAL AND TYRONE NAVIGATION.

These works have been kept in good order during the year, and were handed over to the Directors of the Lagan Navigation Company on the 8th April, 1889,' in accordance with the provisions of the Act of Parliament.

RIVER MAIGUE NAVIGATION.

The works of repair and improvement are in course of execution.

ROYAL UNIVERSITY.

The Board have maintained the fabric of this building in tenantable order.

ANCIENT MONUMENTS PROTECTION ACT, 1882,

45 & 46 Vic., c. 73.

In all cases in which the monuments scheduled in the Act have been handed over to the guardianship of the Commissioners, the necessary steps have been taken for their preservation.

Inspections have been made of a large number of additional structures of a similar character to those scheduled in the Act above referred to, and negotiations have been entered into with the owners of those which are considered of sufficient interest, with the view to these structures being transferred to the guardianship of the Commissioners on terms they can recommend for favourable consideration, and the Board will shortly be in a position to submit a report to their Lordships on the subject.

III.—MISCELLANEOUS OR NON-VOTED SERVICES.

This last division of our duties comprises a variety of services placed under our control or management in pursuance of several Acts of Parliament.

Though numerous, some of them are of only casual occurrence, and therefore do not form the subject of any special remarks.

Those on which special reports follow are arterial drainage works, where, except in the matter of occasional maintenance, our functions, in addition to making loan advances, are confined to advice to Drainage Trustees and Boards, in making awards for completed works, to distribute the proper proportion of charges among the proprietors of land in each district, and, when called upon to do so, to increase the rents of tenants in respect of these improvements.

We are charged with a variety of duties in connexion with fishery piers and harbours which are constructed by Government grants and contributions from counties, and other locally interested in these works. This duty is not confined to new works, but to the very numerous piers which have been constructed from time to time by Government aid since the year 1820, and which, although vested in counties, frequently require the direct interference of Government, either in the matter of repairs or otherwise.

The operations on the service, as the report shows, were largely increased by the grant made by Parliament of £250,000, out of the Irish Church Funds under the provisions of the Sea Fisheries (Ireland) Act, 1883.

The extensive loan operations leads sometimes to the necessity of our taking over and completing works which have been commenced by borrowers, who have failed in their execution.

The administration of the Shannon and other navigations in Ireland, whether maintained from their own funds, as in the case of the Shannon, or partly by votes of Parliament, involve considerable care and attention.

The next class of duties embraced in this division is the administration of two special loan funds, one the Irish Reproductive Loan Fund, including ten distinct funds, applicable to the counties named hereafter in this Report. The funds of the eight maritime counties are applied to the purpose of loans to aid fishermen in buying boats, gear, nets, or in creating oyster beds; and in the case of two inland counties, Roscommon and Tipperary, to works of general utility by any Town Commissioners in these counties.

The Sea and Coast Fisheries Fund, which was handed over to us, in pursuance of an Act passed in 1884, is applicable for Fishery Loans in all the maritime counties of Ireland, a preference being given to those counties which are not in possession of any assignment under the Irish Reproductive Loan Fund.

Another important branch of this division is the care and preservation of 187 National ecclesiastical structures which have been vested in us from time to time, and are maintained out of a grant of £50,000 allocated for the purpose from the Irish Church Fund in pursuance of the Irish Church Act, 1869.

Certain duties in connexion with the Grand Jury system of Ireland still devolve on us, the principal of which are the occasional repair of Post Roads, the examination of County Surveyors' Assistants, the building of bridges between counties, and other miscellaneous duties.

The Report also shows that we are charged with certain duties in connexion with Limited Owners' Residences, Arbitrations under the Railways Acts, and in aiding the Local Government Board with certain financial duties connected with Emigration, Relief of Distress, and also carrying out the duties of the Board of Control of Lunatic Asylums.

A report of the proceedings taken by us in connexion with the Tramways and Light Railways of Ireland, both under former Acts and under the Tramways and Public Companies Act of 1883, is also appended.

The receipts and expenditure incurred under the Miscellaneous Services are detailed in the Appendix A 5, A 6, and A 7, and amount to £114,364 and £114,195 respectively, as against £139,537 and £142,940, in the year to 31st March, 1888.

D

Drainage and Improvement of Lands (Ireland) Act, 1863, and Amendments; 26 & 27 Vic., c. 88; 37 & 38 Vic., c. 72; 28 & 29 Vic., c. 52; 32 & 33 Vic., c. 72; 35 & 36 Vic., c. 31; 37 & 38 Vic., c. 32; 41 & 42 Vic., c. 59; and 43 & 44 Vic., c. 27.

The total number of applications received from the passing of the first of these Acts in the year 1863 to the 31st of March, 1889, is ninety-three.

The preliminary inquiry has been instituted in Tramore River, county Cork, and the Provisional Order constituting this district confirmed by Act of Parliament this Session.

The works have been in progress in the year in the following districts :—

River Suck, counties Galway and Roscommon; Lough and River Erne, Drainage and Navigation, counties of Fermanagh, Cavan, Monaghan, and Donegal; Ballycolliton, county Tipperary; Killard River, county Cork; Cashen River, county Kerry; and Glasheen River, county Cork; and in the following cases the final awards have been made —Owenroe or Moynalty, county Meath; Nanny River, county Meath; Upper Nanny River, county Meath; Upper Morning Star, county Limerick; Ballyteigue and Kilmore, county Wexford; and Follestown, county Meath.

A schedule of the final awards made under these Acts will be found in the Appendix. The total area of land drained or improved in the 49 districts in which final awards have been made, is 87,964 statute acres, and the total cost chargeable thereto amounts to £555,631. This has been in addition to the works of the 121 districts, carried out under the Act 5 & 6 Vic., c. 89, and the Acts amending it, between the years 1843 and 1860, on which an expenditure of £2,390,612 was incurred, of which £70,201 was for works chargeable on counties; £141,078 a free grant; £1,206,812 remitted; and £1,043,227 made repayable by annuity or otherwise, by which 266,736 acres were drained or improved.

Increased Rents in respect of Drainage Charges.

During the past year 4 applications were received from Proprietors for increased rents to be paid by the tenants in respect of lands improved by drainage, embracing 30 holdings; 17 being tenants from year to year, and 13 leaseholders; and meetings have been held by us to determine the amounts.

Drainage Maintenance.

29 & 30 Vic., cap. 49.

One case of maintenance, the Doohyle District, in the county of Limerick, where the works have been completed at a cost of £415 10s.

Railway Clauses Consolidation Act.

8th Vic., c. 20, Sec. 25.

In the following cases the Companies have complied with the requirements of the Act, and the certificates of dimensions of culverts and waterways have been issued :—
Kanturk and Newmarket Railway Company (Banteer to Newmarket).
West Donegal Railway Company (Draminin to Donegal.)

Fishery Piers and Harbours Maintenance.

Under 16 & 17 Vic., c. 136.

During the year no complaint was made of neglect on the part of Grand Juries to maintain the piers handed over to them.

Sea Fisheries (Ireland) Act, 1883.

The total expenditure on this service for works and contingencies to the end of the past year amounts to a sum of £241,264, viz. :—£226,352 to the end of the year 1887-8, and £14,912 during the year 1888-9. This leaves a balance of £8,736 applicable to the completion of the two works now remaining on hand out of the fifty-nine piers and harbours sanctioned from time to time by your Lordships to be constructed out of the sum of £250,000 made available under the Act from the Irish Church funds.

Fifty-one of these works have been completely finished and transferred for future maintenance under warrant to the Grand Juries of their respective counties, six are practically complete, and two others (Passage East and Clogher Head), are still under construction. The last named work while in its unfinished state suffered very serious damage during the heavy storm of last November; we hope, however, that it will be finished within the current year, and without exceeding the limits of the amount originally sanctioned by your Lordships. The amount as above sanctioned under the Act has not only covered the cost of the works already finished, but has also served to meet all expenditure arising from contingencies due to storm damages, and a large sum for additions and improvements to the said works, the construction of which was not originally provided for, but which were found desirable during construction.

Of the fifty-nine works undertaken, thirty-eight were let by contract, and twenty-one were executed by day's labour. The gross estimated cost of those latter works was £34,775; the total expenditure, including a sum of £305 expended in works to give additional accommodation, amounted to £31,941, thus showing a saving of £8,189.

We trust it will be satisfactory to your Lordships to learn that the results now submitted are even more successful than those given five years ago in our 52nd Annual Report, page 26, and the more so as the occurrence of a storm of unprecedented violence and duration last November, has served to demonstrate incontestibly the perfect stability of those structures.

The storm alluded to commenced on the evening of the 1st November, 1888, and up to the 10th inclusive, the registered velocity of the wind at Kingstown was between thirty-five and forty miles per hour. On the 13th and 14th the weather moderated a little, but on the 15th another gale commenced and continued for eleven days, during which the daily maximum velocity ranged between forty-seven and sixty-five miles per hour.

It is particularly satisfactory to have to note that notwithstanding the alarming statements which at the time were made as to the effects of the November gale on the Ballycotton Harbour, not the very slightest injury was sustained during this most severe ordeal. Since the completion of the work in December, 1886, no repairs whatever have been made, nor are any likely to be required; in fact it has been proved, by the only reliable test, to be a perfectly sound marine work, as it has been admitted to be well designed.

On the 19th December last, the District Engineers in charge of the several divisions of the coast, were called upon to visit and report upon the piers in their districts. With the exception of the failure of some concrete pavement at a boat slip in the County Cork, since then shown not to have been due to any unskilfulness in design or execution of work, all the piers visited were reported to be in good order after this crucial test of extreme storm, which it is needless to observe is the only one of the slightest value.

ARKLOW HARBOUR, CO. WICKLOW.

It is nearly a century ago since, under the provisions of an Act of Parliament, this harbour became the property of the Hibernian Mine Company. Between that time and the year 1882, the Company and their successors (The Wicklow Copper Mine Company) expended large sums (stated to amount to between £20,000 and £30,000) on the harbour. In the latter year the Act of Parliament, 45 Vic., cap. 13, was passed, which provided for the transfer of all the rights of the Mining Company to the Board, who were empowered to construct new works at an estimated cost of £85,000, including a sum of £5,000 paid to the Company for their rights.

The works, as originally designed, consisted of a main pier and a wharf 700 feet in length, and a northern groin, parallel to it, 435 feet long, forming with the pier an entrance 170 feet wide; but subsequently, when the main pier was far advanced towards completion, at the urgent and apparently unanimous request of the merchants and traders of Arklow, your Lordships directed that the erection of the groin should not be proceeded with. The total expenditure on the works, including the cost of the concrete blocks for the building of the north groin, all of which are on the ground, amounted to the sum of £35,468 17s. 10d.

The harbour is situated in the Irish Sea, about thirty-five miles south of Kingstown, in a very exposed situation, where the bed of the sea is composed of fine sand about thirty feet deep. During construction considerable damage was done to the South Pier in a south-easterly storm, by the sea tearing away the sandy foundations. All the difficulties, which were considerable, were however successfully overcome, and the foundations have been carefully examined since then after every gale, and especially after the violent storms of last winter, but no injury whatever has been done to the new works.

On the 18th February last, the harbour was handed over to the new authority, constituted under the special Act of Parliament.

The fishermen and traders of Arklow last year submitted a memorial, praying for the erection of the north groin, without which the harbour was incomplete, this groin being, in their opinion, a necessary adjunct to, as they therein term it, this "splendid piece of work, the new extension."

KINSALE HARBOUR.

The works carried out under the provision of 43 & 44 Vic., cap. 174, consist of a pier at the Town Rock, 180 feet long and 100 feet broad; a line of quay about one-third of a mile in length; approach roads from Main Street and Fisher Street, and three boatslips, with other necessary works, the total cost of which was nearly £22,000.

The transfer of these works to the Harbour Commissioners of Kinsale, provided for by Act of Parliament, has been delayed in consequence of an action at law being taken by the Contractor against the Board for extra work. This has now been brought to a close in a satisfactory manner, and the transfer will be made as the legal requirement has been completed.

CLARE SLOB RECLAMATION.

This work has been maintained in good order during the past year, and stood the winter storms without damage; the main embankment has been strengthened and raised, and the surface of the intake raised. Some matters of draining and fencing still require to be done, which are expected to be finished before the 1st December next.

We have issued advertisements (with plan and descriptive particulars) offering the lands for sale. They are situated in the estuary of the River Fergus about six miles from Ennis, the capital and assize town of the County Clare, and about four miles from Clare Castle, the harbour where there is pier accommodation for vessels of 600 tons. The intake consists of about 1,200 acres of very rich alluvial virgin soil, protected by a bank about four miles in length, stone pitched on the sea face.

SHANNON NAVIGATION.

LIMERICK AND UPPER SHANNON.

The works generally have been kept in good order. A pair of new lock-gates were erected at Errina, and a pair of new breast-gates at Killaloe guard lock. It will be necessary to renew the lock-gates at Athlone during the current year.

LOWER SHANNON.

The works at Saleen, Ballylongford, and Foynes are in good order; but at the last-mentioned harbour there is a great accumulation of mud. The original depth cannot be maintained without constant dredging.

LOWER BOYNE NAVIGATION.

The works of this navigation have been maintained in good order during the year.

IRISH REPRODUCTIVE LOAN FUND.

The following statement shows the total amount advanced on loan for fishery purposes (with two exceptions, viz. the purpose, in counties Roscommon and Tipperary, being erection of a Town Hall), in each of the ten counties interested, up to 31st December, 1888, the date of the last Parliamentary return, and the total repayments to the same date :—

County.	No. of Loans.	Total Amount advanced to 31st December, 1888.	Total Amount to be repaid, including interest at the rate of 5½ per cent. per annum.	Repayments to 31st December, 1888.	Balance available for Loan, being Cash Balances and Consols to credit on 1st January, 1889.
		£ s. d.	£ s. d.	£ s. d.	£ s. d.
Clare, . . .	337	4,506 9 0	9,101 4 5	4,605 10 4	2,236 14 10
Cork, . . .	497	20,422 13 10	21,623 18 2	16,080 7 8	1,858 5 7
Galway, . .	1,475	20,323 7 0	27,592 1 1	16,902 9 1	3,868 3 9
Kerry, . . .	765	21,477 4 9	32,636 4 9	20,139 13 5	14,413 7 3
Leitrim, . .	4	100 0 0	108 10 10	108 10 10	2,004 1 7
Limerick, . .	8	502 10 0	681 3 4	307 13 9	3,371 0 0
Mayo, . . .	1,366	11,828 4 0	12,487 17 3	10,223 3 4	2,937 13 5
Sligo, . . .	320	4,957 3 0	5,369 13 7	4,145 9 5	2,172 19 4
Roscommon, .	1	1,500 0 0	1,899 18 0	279 18 0	6,234 15 4
Tipperary, . .	1	1,000 0 0	1,000 0 0	—	3,187 3 6
Total, . .	4,874	87,024 12 7	92,369 11 6	73,592 14 11	42,454 9 7

The above totals include 307 loans for £5,190 made in the year, as compared with 317 loans for £5,075 in the previous year. The repayments in the year amounted to £6,478 as compared with £7,274 in 1886. The arrears of instalments we regret to report have increased from £2,505 to £2,924. £200 of this increase occurred in county Galway, and is attributable to the difficulty experienced in levying decrees; and an increase of £150 occurred in county Cork, which sum represents the arrears on two large loans.

SEA AND COAST FISHERIES FUND.

The following statement shows the total amount advanced on loan for fishery purposes in each of the maritime counties to 31st December, 1888, the date of the last Parliamentary Return, and the total repayments to same date :—

County.	No. of Loans.	Total Amount advanced to 31st December, 1888.	Total Amount to be repaid, including interest at the rate of 2½ per cent. per annum.	Repayments to 31st December, 1888.	Balance available for Loan, being Cash Balances and Consols to credit on 1st January, 1889.
		£ s. d.	£ s. d.	£ s. d.	£ s. d.
General—Loans made by late Trustees, . . .	696	16,780 0 0	17,430 3 9	15,341 1 7	
Antrim, . . .	13	223 18 3	238 14 3	101 1 3	
*Cork, . . .	82	7,801 0 0	8,491 3 11	3,859 6 10	
Donegal, . .	212	3,137 4 10	3,336 19 10	1,521 13 3	
Down, . . .	23	1,925 15 0	2,081 11 7	609 8 3	
Dublin, . . .	37	8,445 10 0	9,236 13 1	3,962 16 10	
*Galway, . .	192	2,409 0 8	2,564 9 0	1,335 12 2	16,842 17 11
Londonderry, .	13	188 0 0	197 7 4	79 14 4	
Louth, . . .	7	536 0 0	594 12 0	66 3 4	
*Mayo, . . .	104	784 5 0	837 3 8	536 18 0	
Meath, . . .	1	10 0 0	10 10 0	8 15 0	
Waterford, . .	14	719 0 0	761 18 2	523 14 4	
Wexford, . .	19	281 0 0	298 17 6	199 19 6	
Wicklow, . .	16	3,322 0 0	3,716 8 4	774 11 2	
Total, . .	1,197	45,561 13 1	49,716 11 7	27,920 15 10	16,842 17 11

This fund is primarily applicable to the necessities of the counties not endowed under the Irish Reproductive Loan Fund. In each of the counties marked * the endowment under that Fund was insufficient to meet the loan requirements of the year, hence the allocation out of the Sea and Coast Fisheries Fund. Sixty-six loans, amounting to £6,218, were advanced during the year, as compared with 100 loans for £8,000 in 1887, and the repayments for the same period amounted to £5,445, as compared with £5,170 for 1887. The arrears stand at £2,501, as compared with £2,466 in the previous year, the greater portion of which are in respect of loans made by the late Trustees.

NATIONAL MONUMENTS AND ECCLESIASTICAL RUINS (IRISH CHURCH ACT, 1869),

32 & 33 Vic., cap. 42, s. 25.

The several works necessary for the preservation of the several structures vested in the Board for preservation as National Monuments have been attended to, and some extensive repairs, which were required for the maintenance of the ruins of the Abbey of St. Francis, at Kilkenny, are now in progress.

POST ROADS.

Act 6 & 7 Wm. IV., cap. 116, section 61.

Applications from the Postmaster-General were received during the past year for repairs of post roads situate in the following counties:—

Co. MAYO.—Westport Post Office to Attyreece Bridge; Bangor to Derrycorrib; Ballaghaderreen to Loughglynn.   Co. DONEGAL.—Malin to Ballygorman.

Where the roads are not already under contract, the repairs are executed under the superintendence of the respective County Surveyors.   The cost of the works is defrayed by the Board, and is repayable by Grand Jury Presentment at subsequent Assizes.

COUNTY SURVEYORS' ASSISTANTS.

Twelve Candidates for the office of County Surveyors' Assistants have been examined under the warrant of the Lord Lieutenant, pursuant to the provisions of the Act 6 & 7 Wm. IV., c. 116, and their qualifications certified to the County Surveyors.

LIMITED OWNERS' RESIDENCES (SETTLED ESTATES ACTS).

27 & 28 Vic., c. 113; 33 & 34 Vic., c. 56; 34 & 35 Vic., c. 84; 40 & 41 Vic., c. 31.

No order has been made under these Acts during the year.

ARBITRATIONS UNDER "THE RAILWAYS (IRELAND) ACTS,"
(1851, 1860, 1864.)

14 & 15 Vic., c. 70; 23 & 24 Vic., c. 97; and 27 & 28 Vic., c. 71.

Arbitrations have been applied for and Arbitrators appointed for the following, viz.:—

Railway Companies:

> The Ballinascarty and Timoleague Junction Light Railway Company—Lands required for undertaking.

> The Dublin, Wicklow, and Wexford Railway Company—Lands required in connection with Diversion Railways [49 Vic., c. 13 (Local)].

> The Midland Great Western of Ireland Railway Company—Additional lands required at Kilbrook, Co. Kildare.

> The Mitchelstown and Fermoy Light Railway Company—Lands required for undertaking.

> The West Donegal Railway Company—Lands required in connection with West Donegal Railway Order, 1886.

> The Great Northern of Ireland Railway Company—Lands required for the purpose of the extension of Dundalk Station.

Commissioners:

The Rathmines and Rathgar Improvement Commissioners—Acquisition of premises known as the "Chains and Streamville," Co. Dublin.

Corporations:

The Corporation of Belfast—Additional Wayleave required in connection with Belfast Main Drainage Act, 1887.

Companies:

The Moore Street Market and North Dublin City Improvement Company— Premises, &c., required.

Boards of Guardians of Poor Law Unions:

North Dublin, Ardee, Mitchelstown, Schull, Delvin, Ennistymon, Tulla, Enniscorthy, Cashel, Mountmellick, Edenderry, Skibbereen—Lands required for the purposes of the Labourers (Ireland) Acts, 46 & 47 Vic., c. 60, and 48 & 49 Vic., c. 77.

Cavan—Lands, &c., required in connection with Cavan Waterworks.

TRAMWAYS AND LIGHT RAILWAYS.

TRAMWAYS ACTS, 23 & 24 Vic., c. 152 (1860); 24 & 25 Vic., c. 102 (1861); 34 & 35 Vic., c. 114 (1871); 44 & 45 Vic., c. 17 (1881), and 46 & 47 Vic., c. 43 (1883).

Under the provisions of the Tramways Acts of 1860 and 1861 we are required, on the application of the promoters of tramway and light railway projects, to cause an inquiry to be held into the merits of the undertakings from an engineering point of view, and to any modification in that respect which may be advantageously made, and to report our opinion thereon. These reports are directed to be submitted to the Grand Juries for their consideration in approving of the proposals made, prior to granting a baronial guarantee on the amount of capital required for the carrying out of any proposed undertaking, and to an Order of the Lord Lieutenant in Council being sought.

The cost of these inquiries has been defrayed out of funds deposited in our hands by the Promoters.

The following cases were brought forward for inquiry at last Summer and Spring Assizes, and were duly reported on by the Board :—Macroom and Ballyvourney; Midleton, Cloyne, and Ballycottin; Baltimore Extension; Limerick, Bruff and Kilmallock; South Clare; Tralee and Dingle (Deviations); and the Timoleague and Courtmacsherry, and Newcastle and Buttevant, of which the two last named received the requisite guarantee on their capital.

Our duty in connexion with guaranteed undertakings is that prescribed by the 10th section, subsection 4, of the Tramways Act of 1883, which enacts that before any Order in Council is made authorizing the carrying out of a guaranteed project, we are required to furnish the Lord Lieutenant in Council with an estimate of the amount of paid-up capital which will be necessary for the purposes of the undertaking. The estimates having been examined and checked for that purpose, are submitted to the Privy Council at the hearing of applications for Orders authorizing the construction of any line of tramway or light railway, and the Engineers who checked those estimates attend at the hearing and are examined thereon. The following table shows the applications which have been passed by the Privy Council under this Act, together with the valuation of guaranteeing areas, &c., &c. :—

The total mileage of projects guaranteed is 260 miles, viz. (see Nos. I., II., and III. in following list), and the guaranteed capital £1,064,000. The orders have lapsed in five other cases, amounting to £205,648, detailed at IV.

GUARANTEED UNDERTAKINGS passed by PRIVY COUNCIL.

I.—CONSTRUCTED AND OPENED TO THE PUBLIC.

Name of Project.	No. of Miles.	Promoters' Estimate.	Board's Estimate.	Amount of Guarantee.	Guaranteeing Area.		
		£	£	£	County.	Baronies.	Valuation. £
Carrickfergus Harbour Junction Light Railway.	1	7,500	7,500	5,000	Antrim,	Co. of Town of Carrickfergus,	20,007 0 0
Cavan, Leitrim, and Roscommon Light Railway.	48	261,000	234,000	62,500 154,000	Cavan, Leitrim,	Parts of Loughtee Lower, Tullyhaw, Tullyhaw, Carrigallen, and Leitrim and Mohill.	57,276 0 0
West Clare Light Railway,	27	189,000	170,000	166,400	Clare,	All Baronies,	316,735 0 0
Ballinascarty and Timoleague Light Railway.	6	28,500	31,000	25,000	Cork,	Ibane and Barryroe, and E. Carbery, E. D. (part).	43,574 0 0
Cork, Coachford, and Blarney Light Railway.	15	78,000	74,100	75,000	" "	Parts of E. Muskerry, Cork, and Barretts.	52,000 0 0
Schull and Skibbereen Light Railway.	14	57,000	61,000	57,000	" "	West Carbery, W.D., E.D.	61,000 0 0
Ogilla and Blessington Steam Tramway.	15	60,000	65,000	60,000	Dublin and Wicklow.	Parts of Rathdown, Upper-cross, Newcastle, and Talbotstown.	30,000 0 0
Clogher Valley Tramway,	36	125,325	146,000	152,000	Fermanagh and Tyrone.	Parts of Magheraboy, Tyrkennedy, Lower Dungannon, and Clogher.	59,570 0 0
	162			£781,800			

II.—LINES IN PROGRESS OF CONSTRUCTION.

Name of Project.	No. of Miles.	Promoters' Estimate.	Board's Estimate.	Amount of Guarantee.	County.	Baronies.	Valuation.
Mitchelstown and Fermoy Light Railway.	12	63,000	63,000	63,000	Cork,	Condons and Clongibbons, and Fermoy (part).	73,843 0 0
West Donegal Light Railway	4	15,000	20,000	15,000	Donegal,	Parts of Tyrhugh and Banagh,	26,132 0 0
Tralee and Dingle Light Railway,	37	133,000	134,000	133,000	Kerry,	Corkaguiny, Clanmaurice, Trughanacmy (part), and Urban Sanitary District of Tralee.	143,317 0 0
Timoleague and Courtmacsherry,	9	15,700	12,000	22,000	Cork,	Ibane and Barryroe, and E. Carbery, E.D. (part of).	42,521 15 0
	62			£211,000			

III.—LINES NOT COMMENCED BUT ORDERS STILL VALID.

Name of Project.	No. of Miles.	Promoters' Estimate.	Board's Estimate.	Amount of Guarantee.	County.	Baronies.	Valuation.
Armagh and Keady Light Railway.	9	67,000	55,000	60,000	Armagh,	Tiranny, Upper Fews, and Lower Fews.	66,638 0 0
West Kerry Light Railway,	27	123,000	147,000	112,000	Kerry,	Iveragh,	19,806 0 0
	36			£177,000			
Total I., II., and III.,	260			£1,064,000			

IV.—LINES WHERE THE ORDERS HAVE EXPIRED.

Name of Project.	No. of Miles.	Promoters' Estimate.	Board's Estimate.	Amount of Guarantee.	County.	Baronies.	Valuation.
Kilrush and Kilkee Light Railway,	5	40,000	40,000	40,000	Clare,	Moyarta,	31,677 0 0
Woodlawn and Mount Bellew Tramway.	9	33,000	36,000	31,500	Galway,	Parts of Ballymoe, Killian, Tiaquin, Kilconnel.	42,654 0 0
Loughrea and Attymon Light Railway.	9	52,000	60,700	54,448		Parts of Leitrim, Dunkellin, Athenry, Kilconnell, Loughrea, Longford, and Tiaquin.	254,497 0 0
Shillelagh and Newtownbarry Light Railway.	11	40,953	61,700	42,000	Wicklow, Wexford, and Carlow.	Shillelagh, Scarawalsh, and parts of St. Mullins Upper, and Forth.	25,704 0 0
Newtownbarry and Scarawalsh Light Railway.	9	25,395	45,000	25,000	Wexford,	Scarawalsh,	46,916 0 0
	43			£205,945			

An Order in Council being sought authorizing deviations in the Tralee and Dingle Light Railway, we duly reported on them.

An amount is provided in the Estimates to enable us to meet any contributions which may become payable in respect of the two per cent. guaranteed by Government under the 9th Section of the "Tramways (Ireland) Act, 1883."

RECEIVER ACCOUNTS FOR LOANS.

We continue in possession of the Southern and the Letterkenny Railway. The gross earnings of the Southern Railway in the year 1888 amounted to £8,976, and after paying for haulage, rent to the Great Southern, and other charges, there remained a surplus of £1,720. We received from the County Tipperary and the individual guarantors the sum of £3,145, to pay the half-yearly dividend at the rate of 5 per cent. per annum on the guaranteed stock amounting to £62,900, which has been duly paid over to the shareholders holding that Stock. The gross receipts of the Letterkenny Railway in the year 1888 amounted to £5,358, as compared with £4,926 in 1887, the surplus revenue being £1,411.

Our Receiver over the Galway Harbour Revenues reports a gross receipt in the year to 31st March last of £3,139 5s. 9d. We paid over to the Exchequer in the same time £922, the balance of £2,207 5s. 9d. being required to meet the cost of renewing the dock gates.

We have the honour to be

Your Lordships' obedient Servants,

R. H. SANKEY.

W. R. LE FANU.

S. U. ROBERTS.

Commissioners of Public Works
in Ireland.

W. R. SOADY, *Secretary,*

 Office of Public Works,

  Dublin, 29th June, 1889.

APPENDIX A.—

(A.)—Abstract of the Accounts of the Commissioners of Public Works in Ireland, showing the Total of

No.	Page	Heads of Account.	Balances on 31st March, 1888.	Received.
			£ s. d.	£ s. d.
A 1	36	Parliamentary Votes and Grants, viz.:—		
		1. Public Buildings, Royal Harbours, &c.,		
		2. Museum of Science and Art,		
		3. Office of Public Works,	7,625 13 10	255,204 1 7
		4. Exchequer—Extra Receipts.		
A 2	42	Loans Advances,	43,968 5 6	450,000 0 0
A 3	44	Loans Repayments,	—	788,565 14 5
A 4	44	Land Improvement Preliminaries, 10 Vic. c. 32,	155 6 11	1,776 0 5
A 5	46	District Lunatic Asylums,	2,549 7 8	23,644 8 6
A 6	46	Sea Fisheries, Ireland, 46 & 47 Vic. c. 26,	4,890 3 4	21,496 16 8
A 7	46	Miscellaneous Services, viz.:—		
		1. Deposit Accounts, 1 & 2 Wm. IV. c. 62, &c.,		
		2. Railway and other Arbitrations, 14 & 15 Vic. c. 70,		
		3. Arterial Drainage Deposits, 26 & 27 Vic. c. 88, &c.,		
		4. Inland Navigations:—Shannon,		
		5. Drainage Maintenance, 29 & 30 Vic. c. 68,		
		6. Shannon Drainage—Special Works,		
		7. National Monuments, 32 & 33 Vic. c. 42,		
		8. Linen Hall,		
		9. Irish Reproductive Loan Fund, 27 & 28 Vic. c. 86,	7,295 17 8	67,447 0 2
		10. Sea and Coast Fisheries Loan Fund,		
		11. Kinsale Harbour,		
		12. Arklow Harbour Maintenance,		
		13. Clare Bleb Reclamation,		
		14. Galway Harbour Receiver's Account,		
		15. Southern Railway,		
		16. Letterkenny Railway,		
		17. Emigration Grants,		
		18. Sundry Accounts,		
		Total.	66,628 14 0	1,727,117 1 7
A 8	56	Statement of Final Awards under Arterial Drainage Act, 26 & 27 Vic. c. 68, with Repayments thereon, to the 31st March, 1889.		

Office of Public Works, Dublin, 30th April, 1889.

ACCOUNTS.

Sums intrusted to their Management for Collection or Disbursement for One Year, ended on 31st March, 1889.

Balances overdrawn, 31st March, 1888.	Totals.	Overdrawn Balances from Accounts to 31st March, 1888.	Paid.	Balances on 31st March, 1889.	Totals.
£ s. d.	£ s. d.	£ s. d.	£ s. d.	£ s. d.	£ s. d.
—	500,869 15 5	—	282,214 4 0	18,655 11 5	500,869 15 5
—	893,988 5 8	—	857,021 13 8	36,966 12 0	893,988 5 8
—	769,648 14 8	—	769,648 14 5	—	769,648 14 5
—	1,929 7 4	—	1,689 12 6	459 14 10	1,929 7 4
—	26,193 16 0	—	25,082 10 5	1,141 5 7	26,193 16 0
—	26,277 0 0	—	22,912 7 7	3,364 12 5	26,277 0 0
—	74,843 17 8	—	64,680 7 1	10,162 10 7	74,843 17 8
—	1,793,749 16 4	—	1,722,979 9 6	70,770 6 10	1,793,740 16 4

Geo. Pearse, Accountant.

E 2

An Account showing the Receipts and Expenditure of the Commissioners

(A 1.)—PARLIAMENTARY

RECEIPTS.	£ s. d.	£ s. d.	£ s. d.
Balance from the last Account, ...	—	—	7,565 13 10
I. PUBLIC BUILDINGS.			
Vote for the year 1888–89, ...	—	196,302 0 0	
NEW WORKS AND ALTERATIONS :—			
Transfer from Sub-head "Maintenance," . .	—	3 9 5	
Carried forward, . . .	—	196,305 9 5	7,565 13 10

of Public Works in the Year ended 31st March, 1889.

VOTES AND GRANTS.

EXPENDITURE.	£ s. d.	£ s. d.	£ s. d.
Balances on Parliamentary Votes, 1887–88, surrendered to H.M. Exchequer, viz.:—			
Public Buildings,	—	5,259 14 5	
Royal University,	—	11 1 4	
Science and Art Buildings,	—	30 17 0	
Office of Public Works, .	—	1,572 15 4	6,874 5 2
1. PUBLIC BUILDINGS.			
NEW WORKS AND ALTERATIONS:—			
Coastguard Buildings, .	2,831 17 11		
Naval Reserve Buildings,	1,113 5 4		
Ordnance Survey Office, .	751 0 6		
General Valuation Office,	380 4 10		
Land Commission Office,	140 9 0		
Dublin Metropolitan Police Buildings,	636 9 9		
Constabulary Buildings, .	5,135 8 8		
Dundrum Criminal Lunatic Asylum,	231 11 6		
Science and Art Buildings, .	228 11 11		
National Education Buildings:—	£ s. d.		
Ordinary Literary Schools, .	41,495 3 5		
Teachers' Residences,	230 0 0	41,725 3 5	
Customs Buildings, .	1,367 16 7		
Postal and Telegraph Buildings,	1,735 16 11	56,954 15 10	
Carried forward, .	—	56,954 15 10	6,874 5 2

An Account showing the Receipts and Expenditure of the Commissioners

(A 1.)—PARLIAMENTARY

RECEIPTS—continued.

	£ s. d.	£ s. d.	£ s. d.
brought forward, . .	—	195,305 9 5	7,665 13 10
1. Public Buildings—continued.			
Transfers and Repayments:—			
Maintenance and Supplies, ...	36 8 0		
Furniture, Fittings, &c., ...	3 16 0		
Fuel, Light, Water, &c., ...	0 5 10		
		39 9 10	
			195,344 19 3
Carried forward, ...	—	—	205,010 13 1

of PUBLIC WORKS in the Year ended 31st March, 1889—continued.

VOTES AND GRANTS—continued.

EXPENDITURE—continued.

	Maintenance and Supplies.	Pensions, Fittings, and Utensils.	Rent and Insurance.	Fuel, Light, Water, Cleaning, &c.	Total.		
	£ s. d.	£ s. d.	£ s. d.	£ s. d.	£ s. d.	£ s. d.	£ s. d.
Brought forward, .	—	—	—	—	—	58,954 15 10	6,574 8 2
PUBLIC BUILDINGS—con.							
Royal Hospital, Kilmainham,							
Royal Hibernian Military School,							
Quartermaster-General's Office,							
Constabulary Buildings,							
Ord. Survey, Mountjoy Barrack,							
Dublin Castle Buildings,							
Under Secretary's House,							
Viceregal Lodge, Gardens, &c.,							
Private Secretary's Lodge,							
Chief Sec's Lodge, Gardens, &c.,							
Under Sec't. Lodge and Demesne,							
Chief Sec's Office and Branches,							
Board of Trade Survey Office,							
Civil Service Commission, .							
Paymaster-General's Office, .							
Stationery Office, Marion-street,							
Quit Rent Offices, Ormond-quay,							
Postal Inspection Office,							
Charitable Bequests Office,							
Local Government Board, .							
Office of Public Works,							
Record Room and Offices,							
General Registry & Census Offices,							
General Survey & Valuation Office,							
Depot for Crown Witnesses,							
High Court of Justice, Four Courts,							
Court of Bankruptcy,							
King's Inns:—Registry of Deeds,							
District Probate Registry Offices,							
Registry of Judgments,							
Land Com. Court and Offices,							
Met. Police Courts and Offices,							
Metropolitan Police Stations,							
Divisional Magistrates' Offices,							
Royal Irish Con. Depot & Offices,							
Con. Barracks throughout Ireland,							
General Prisons Office,							
Reformatory and Industrial Schools Office,							
Dundrum Crim. Lunatic Asylum,							
School of Art, Museum, &c.							
Kildare-street,							
Botanic Gardens, Glasnevin,							
Royal College of Science,							
Geological Survey Office,							
Nat. Educ.—Metropol Buildings,							
Agricultural Model Schools, and Albert Model Farm,							
District and Minor Model Schools							
Ordinary Literary Schools,							
Teachers' Residences,							
Teachers' Pension Office,							
National Gallery of Ireland,							
Queen's College, Cork, .							
" Belfast,							
" Galway,							
Royal Irish Academy,							
Customs Buildings,							
Inland Revenue Buildings,							
Post Office Buildings,							
Telegraph Buildings,							
Phœnix Park,							
St. Stephen's Green Park,							
Curragh of Kildare,							
Kingstown Harbour,							
Howth Harbour,							
Donaghadee Harbour,							
Dunmore Harbour,							
Ardglass Harbour,							
Tyrone Navigation,							
Maigue Navigation,							
Boyne Navigation,							
Ulster Canal, .							
Shannon Navigation—Sluices,							
Endowed Schools Commission,							
Public Works (Ireland) Com. ,							
Ancient Monuments Preservation,							
Royal University,							
Phœnix Park National School,							
Total, . .	27,081 5 4	18,815 1 7	21,129 1 6	7,489 0 0	121,883 19 8	121,993 19 5	

An Account showing the Receipts and Expenditure of the Commissioners

(A 1.)—PARLIAMENTARY

RECEIPTS—continued.	£ s. d.	£ s. d.	£ s. d.
Brought forward,	—	—	206,010 13 1
Public Buildings—continued.			
2. Dublin Museum of Science and Art, and National Library:—			
Vote,	—	—	42,500 0 0
3. Office of Public Works (Class II.):—			
Vote,	—	41,728 0 0	
Law Costs and Stamp Duty recovered,	—	103 7 7	
Transfers and Re-Lodgments,	—	124 17 9	
			41,956 5 4
4. Exchequer Extra Receipts:—			
Public Buildings:—			
Rents,	4,005 14 2		
Sales, &c.,	596 2 8		
		4,601 16 10	
Phoenix and St. Stephen's Green Parks, &c.:—			
Rents for Grazing, &c.,	446 4 2		
Sales,	21 0 0		
		467 4 2	
Kingstown Harbour:—			
Dues,	1,333 17 1		
Rents,	363 12 5		
Water supplied to Shipping,	60 4 6		
Ballast,	63 0 10		
Hire of Planks, Cranes,	21 14 0		
Boat Licenses,	2 10 0		
		1,844 18 10	
Howth Harbour:—			
Dues,	123 7 6		
Sales &c.,	9 16 6		
Rents,	243 19 0		
		377 3 0	
Donaghadee Harbour:—			
Rents,	—	14 3 2	
Ardglass Harbour:—			
Rents,	8 16 0		
Dues,	170 9 5		
Sales,	3 16 5		
		178 1 10	
Dunmore Harbour:—			
Rents,	25 5 8		
Dues,	19 7 6		
Sales,	2 0 0		
		46 13 2	
Tyrone Navigation:—			
Tolls,	281 5 0		
Rents,	47 19 2		
		329 4 2	
Malgue Navigation:—			
Tolls,	—	11 15 2	
Ulster Canal:—			
Tolls,	113 7 6		
Rents,	122 6 7		
		235 14 1	
Boyne Navigation:—			
Tolls,	157 18 6		
Rents,	0 5 0		
		158 3 6	
Salaries, &c. (Class II.),	—	2,137 19 1	
			10,402 17 0
			300,869 15 5

of Public Works in the Year ended 31st March, 1889.

VOTES AND GRANTS—continued.

EXPENDITURE—continued.	£ s. d.	£ s. d.	£ s. d.
Brought forward, . .	—	178,948 15 3	6,874 8 9
PUBLIC BUILDINGS—continued.			
Repayments to Baronies. Tramways and Public Companies (Ireland) Act, 1883, . .	—	5,820 4 5	
Royal University, Ireland, Buildings, . .	—	130 0 0	
Contribution to National Schools, . .	—	—	181,508 10 8
			0 3 11
2. DUBLIN MUSEUM OF SCIENCE AND ART, AND NATIONAL LIBRARY :—			
Buildings, Superintendence, &c., .	—	—	39,187 15 6
3. OFFICE OF PUBLIC WORKS (CLASS II.) :—			
Salaries, ...	—	26,766 15 5	
Travelling Expenses, . .	—	2,651 11 0	
Fees to Counsel, . .	—	595 14 11	
Incidental Expenses, . .	—	222 9 11	
Land Improvement and Land Law Act, Salaries,	—	10,378 15 6	
Irrecoverable Expenses incurred on Local Loans Fund,	—	92 3 4	
			40,710 9 10
4. EXCHEQUER, EXTRA RECEIPTS :—			
Public Buildings :—			
Taxes refunded, . . .	—	8 9 10	
Phœnix Park :—			
Veterinary Inspection, .	—	80 0 0	
Kingstown Harbour :—			
Ballast for Shipping, . .	—	99 4 9	
Howth Harbour :—			
Taxes refunded, . . .	—	1 18 5	
Salaries :—			
Deposits refunded, Land Law Act, sec. 31 .	—	33 0 0	
Transferred to H. M. Exchequer, . .	—	10,602 15 11	10,579 6 11
Balance, . .	—	—	18,655 11 5
			300,869 15 5

(A 2.)—An Account showing the Receipts and Expenditure of the Commissioners

PUBLIC WORKS LOAN

	£ s. d.	£ s. d.
To Balance, 31st March, 1888,	—	43,988 5 5
„ Public Works Loans:—		
Vote of Credit 1887-88, £1,000,000—National Debt Commissioners,	200,000 0 0	
„ 1888-89, £1,000,000—National Debt Commissioners,	350,000 0 0	
		550,000 0 0
		593,988 5 5

Office of Public Works, Dublin, 30th April, 1889.

of PUBLIC WORKS in the Year ended 31st March, 1889.

ADVANCES.

	£ s. d.	£ s. d.
By Public Works Loans,		
Amount advanced on Loans, viz. :—		
Grand Juries of Counties,	3,625 11 9	
Local Boards,	26,400 0 0	
Inland Navigation,	3,500 0 0	
Public Buildings,	—	
Railways,	24,700 0 0	
Harbours, Docks, &c.,	3,315 0 0	
Reclamation of Waste Lands,	1,500 0 0	
Labourers' Dwellings in Towns, 29 & 30 Vic., c. 44,	—	
Housing of the Working Classes,	19,803 0 0	
Glebe Loans, 33 & 34 Vic., c. 112,	11,039 8 8	
Public Health, 37 & 38 Vic., c. 93,	74,471 14 4	
Drainage Maintenance, 29 & 30 Vic., c. 49, &c.,	415 10 0	
District Drainage Boards, 26 & 27 Vic., c. 88,	31,806 0 0	
Post Roads, for Repairs, 6 & 7 Wm. IV., c. 116,	621 6 6	
Land Improvement Preliminary Expenses,	1,000 0 0	
Repairs of Fishery Piers,		
Maintenance of Navigation Works,		
Lunatic Asylums Buildings, 1 & 2 Geo. IV., c. 33,	23,639 8 4	
Emigration,	—	
Labourers' Acts,	242,597 1 5	
Land Improvement, 10 Vic., c. 32, &c.,	31,773 4 6	
National School Teachers' Residences,	12,453 10 0	
Dispensary Houses,	6,788 0 0	
Non-Vested Schools and Training Colleges,	3,233 0 0	
Land Law, 44 & 45 Vic., c. 49, s. 31,	33,641 0 0	557,021 13 6
Balance unissued.	—	36,966 12 0
		593,988 5 6

(A 3.)—An Account showing the Receipts and Expenditure of the Commissioners

PUBLIC WORKS LOANS

	Repayments			Totals.		
	£	s.	d.	£	s.	d.
To Public Works Loans :—						
Amounts received in repayment :—						
Grand Juries of Counties,	11,741	6	8			
Local Boards,	7,596	7	0			
Roads and Bridges,	10,507	11	8			
Inland Navigations,	2,785	17	2			
Public Buildings,	8,058	18	2			
Railways,	80,081	10	1			
Quarries, Mines, and Miscellaneous,	58	1	7			
Harbours, Docks, &c.,	16,598	18	6			
Fishery Piers and Harbours,	689	5	8			
Reclamation of Waste Lands,						
Labourers' Dwellings in Towns,	11,063	16	11			
Artizans' Dwellings,	4,515	5	11			
Housing of the Working Classes,	7,894	3	7			
Globe Loans,	31,115	8	1			
Public Health,	208,012	8	6			
River Drainage and Navigation, 5 & 6 Vic., c. 89,	948	3	9			
River Drainage Maintenance, 29 & 30 Vic., c. 49, &c.,	2,586	18	4			
River Drainage, 26 & 27 Vic., c. 88,	35,601	8	5			
Loans per Act 57 Geo. III., c. 34,	180	0	0			
Port Roads, Repairs,	166	18	9			
Land Improvement Preliminary Expenses,	817	4	1			
Repairs of Fishery Piers,	916	6	9			
Maintenance of Navigation Works,						
Lunatic Asylums Buildings,	27,034	18	4			
Building Schools,	24	14	0			
Relief of Distress,	299	19	2			
Seed Supply,	12,071	1	2			
Emigration,	1,043	1	0			
Labourers' Acts,	20,626	17	6			
Land Improvement Loans,	147,583	14	9			
National School Teachers' Residences,	3,941	15	2			
Dispensary Houses,	8,514	13	8			
Non-Vested Schools and Training Colleges,	887	14	1			
Land Law, 44 & 45 Vic., c. 49, c. 51,	40,389	17	9			
Land Act Loans, 33 & 34 Vic., c. 46,	19,270	12	3	711,112	19	3
Church Fund Loans :—						
Land Improvement,	35,811	15	11			
Sanitary,	1,703	10	5			
Baronial Works,	19,890	15	3			
Relief of Distress,	960	14	6			
Arterial Drainage,	68	19	1	58,435	15	2
				769,548	14	5

Office of Public Works, Dublin, 30th April, 1889.

(A 4.)—LAND IMPROVEMENT

RECEIPTS.	£	s.	d.	£	s.	d.
Balance from last Account,	—			153	6	11
Amount received from National Debt Commissioners by way of Loan,	1,000	0	0			
,, ,, from Proprietors in Repayment of Preliminary Expenses,	776	0	5	1,776	0	5
				1,929	7	4

Office of Public Works, Dublin, 30th April, 1889.

of PUBLIC WORKS, in the Year ended 31st March, 1889.

REPAYMENTS.

	£ s. d.	£ s. d.
By transfers to National Debt Commissioners,	—	711,112 19 3
By transfers to Irish Land Commissioners, .	—	58,435 15 2
		769,548 14 5

GEO. PIRRIE, *Accountant.*

PRELIMINARIES, 1888–89.

EXPENDITURE.	£ s. d.	£ s. d.
Amount paid to National Debt Commissioners in Repayment of Advances, .	817 4 1	
„ paid for Preliminary Investigations, Advertising, Scrivenary, &c., .	652 8 5	
		1,469 12 6
Balance carried to next Account, ...	—	439 14 10
		1,939 7 4

GEO. PIRRIE, *Accountant.*

(A 5.)—LUNATIC

An Account showing the Receipts and Expenditure by the Commissioners of Public Works, Ireland, (on 1889, pursuant to Act 1 & 2

RECEIPTS.	£ s. d.	£ s. d.	£ s. d.
Balance from last Account,	—	—	2,849 7 8
Amount received from the Public Works Loan Fund on account of Loans to the following District Asylums :—			
Ballinasloe,	—	1,854 18 11	
Castlebar,	—	1,000 0 0	
Clonmel,	—	1,000 0 0	
Cork,	—	1,999 4 9	
Enniscorthy,	—	46 16 0	
Killarney,	—	3,500 0 0	
Limerick,	—	540 0 0	
Londonderry,	—	116 11 2	
Monaghan,	2,000 0 0		
Sale of Boiler,	5 0 0		
		2,005 0 0	
Mullingar,	—	750 0 0	
Richmond,	—	10,000 0 0	
Waterford,	—	1,531 17 6	
			23,644 8 4
			26,193 16 0

Office of Public Works, Dublin, 30th April, 1889.

(A 6.)—SEA FISHERIES

An Account showing the Receipts and Expenditure by the Commissioners of Public Works

RECEIPTS.	£ s. d.	£ s. d.	£ s. d.
Balance from last Account,	—	—	4,880 3 4
Amount received from the Land Law Commissioners on account of Grant of £250,000,	—	20,000 0 0	
Amount received in repayment of Loan—			
Ballynagaul Pier—Principal,	28 18 0		
" Interest,	4 0 4		
		33 16 4	
Lisnaunor Harbour—Principal,	54 0 1		
" Interest,	16 7 5		
		70 7 5	
Kilkee Boat-slip—Principal,	9 12 6		
" Interest,	2 12 0		
		12 4 6	
Annalong Harbour—Principal,	27 10 10		
" Interest,	8 16 11		
		36 7 9	
Kilkeel Harbour—Principal,	122 2 8		
" Interest,	36 11 0		
		158 13 8	
Culdaff Pier—Principal,	19 19 1		
" Interest,	5 12 1		
		25 11 2	
Port Salon Pier—Principal,	79 7 8		
" Interest,	22 11 0		
		101 18 8	
Ballydavid Boat-slip—Principal,	33 18 0		
" Interest,	9 3 4		
		43 1 4	
Portstewart Harbour—Principal,	58 16 6		
" Interest,	15 14 6		
		74 10 0	
Amount received as Contribution in aid of Ballynatray Harbour,	—	300 0 0	
Sundry Sales and Refunds,	—	641 5 9	
			21,496 16 8
			26,377 0 0

Office of Public Works, Dublin, 30th April, 1889.

ASYLUMS BUILDINGS.

Account of the Commissioners for the Central, &c., of Lunatic Asylums) during the year ended 31st March.
Geo. IV., c. 33, &c., &c.

EXPENDITURE.	£ s. d.	£ s. d.	£ s. d.
Amounts expended on the following District Asylums, viz.:—			
Ballinasloe,	—	1,344 14 4	
Castlebar,	—	100 1 0	
Clonmel,	—	936 0 6	
Cork,	—	2,174 8 9	
Ennismorthy,	—	54 17 6	
Killarney,	—	3,977 17 3	
Limerick,	—	309 18 2	
Londonderry,	—	9 10 2	
Monaghan,	—	2,863 3 4	
Mullingar,	—	1,066 9 2	
Richmond, Dublin.	—	10,835 18 3	
Waterford,	—	1,611 17 0	
			25,052 10 5
Balance,	—	—	1,141 5 7
			26,193 16 0

(IRELAND) COMMISSION.

IRELAND, during the Year ended 31st March, 1889, pursuant to Act 46 & 47 Victoria, cap. 26.

EXPENDITURE.	£ s. d.	£ s. d.	£ s. d.
Expenses of Engineering Staff, .	—	2,061 13 3	
Amounts expended on the following Works:—			
Inishcrone Pier,	1,077 1 11		
Carlingford Harbour,	5 5 0		
Ross Pier,	33 15 0		
Achill Viaduct Pier,	64 4 0		
Passage East Harbour,	1,635 8 6		
Ballywilliam Harbour,	130 0 6		
Castletown Barehaven Pier,	9 13 10		
Cheek Point Pier,	35 14 3		
Boatstrand Breakwater,	131 19 4		
Trawndaleen Pier,	111 18 10		
Ballycotton Harbour,	87 3 9		
Carrigaholt Harbour,	250 9 1		
Malla Head Harbour,	304 18 5		
Lacken Pier,	552 15 0		
Union Hall Pier,	341 8 10		
Clogher Head Breakwater,	3,940 14 3		
Angeris Pier,	78 15 10		
Portstewart Harbour,	36 0 0		
Brandon Pier,	777 2 11		
Belmullet East Pier,	573 5 7		
Claggan Pier,	1,400 0 10		
Kilmore Harbour,	3,318 16 4		
Greystones Harbour,	3,963 0 2		
Ballyhalbert Pier,	1,432 0 9		
Bundoran Boat Harbour,	223 14 6		
		20,950 15 4	
			23,012 7 7
Balance,	—	—	3,364 12 5
			26,377 0 0

An Account showing the Receipts and Expenditure by the Commissioners

(A 7.)—MISCELLANEOUS

RECEIPTS.	£ s. d.	£ s. d.	£ s. d.
To Balance from last Account, . . .	—	—	7,395 17 6
1. Deposit Accounts for Loans, &c. :— Received from Sundries for Preliminary Expenses,	—	—	1,365 10 9
2. Railway and other Arbitration Expenses, 14 & 15 Vic., c. 70 :— Received from Railway Companies and others, to meet Expenses of Arbitration, . . .	—	—	1,940 10 9
3. Arterial Drainage Deposits, 26 & 27 Vic., c. 88, &c. :— Received from Drainage Boards on Account of Preliminary and other Expenses, ...	—	—	52 5 0
4. Inland Navigations :— Shannon :— Rents, ...	—	2,954 14 1	
Tolls, ...	—	1,738 1 4	
Sales, Refunds, &c., ...	—	177 9 8	4,870 5 1
5. Maintenance of Drainage Works, 29 & 30 Vic., c. 49 :— Doobyle District, ...	—	—	418 8 1
6. Shannon Drainage—Special Works :— From Chief Secretary from Vote 3, Class VII. Public Works and Industries, Ireland, 1888-1889, . .	—	18,035 0 0	
Refund for unpaid labour, &c.—Killaloe, . .	—	15 8 10	
Do. Lough Allen, . .	—	36 19 11	18,067 8 9
7. National Monuments, 32 & 33 Vic., c. 42 — Dividends on Stock, ...	—	—	1,041 18 1
8. Linen Hall :— Rents, ...	—	—	443 4 8
Carried forward, . . .	—	—	35,500 13 5

of Public Works, Ireland, during the Year ended 31st March, 1889.

SERVICES.

EXPENDITURE	£ s. d.	£ s. d.	£ s. d
1. Deposit Accounts for Loans, &c.:— Paid to Sundries for Preliminary Expenses,	—	—	1,816 1 1
2. Railway and other Arbitration Expenses, 14 & 15 Vic., c. 70:— Paid to Valuators, &c.,	—	—	2,661 2 7
3. Arterial Drainage Deposits, 26 & 27 Vic., c. 88, &c.:— Paid for Preliminary Expenses, Arbitrations, &c.,	—	—	29 19 4
4. Inland Navigation:— Shannon:— Maintenance and Repairs of Works,	—	1,976 14 6	
Superintendence,	—	1,260 17 1	
Repayment of Clare Castle Pier Loan,	—	807 6 5	
Compensation, Law Costs, &c.,	—	845 11 8	
Refund of Rates and Income Tax,	—	151 0 0	4,561 7 6
5. Maintenance of Drainage Works, 29 & 30 Vic., c. 49:— Doohyle District,	—	—	389 12 9
6. Shannon Drainage—Special Works:— Killaloe,	—	10,692 5 8	
Lough Allen,	—	4,112 8 2	14,804 13 10
7. National Monuments, 32 & 33 Vic., c. 42:— Maintenance— Salary and Travelling Expenses of Architects; Caretakers' Wages, Incidents, &c.,	—	448 8 9	
Restoration— Ardmore,	8 2 6		
Dromore,	20 0 0		
Holycross,	17 0 9		
Hoare,	18 2 9	64 6 0	512 14 9
8. Linen Hall:— Rent, Salary, &c.,	—	185 16 4	
Transfer to Her Majesty's Exchequer,	—	250 0 0	435 16 4
Carried forward,	—	—	25,711 6 4

G

An Account showing the Receipts and Expenditure of the Commissioners

MISCELLANEOUS

RECEIPTS—continued.	£ s. d.	£ s. d.	£ s. d.
Brought forward, . .	—	—	35,500 13 6
9. IRISH REPRODUCTIVE LOAN FUND, 37 & 38 Vic., c. 86, &c. :—	Dividends on Stock, &c.	Repayments.	
County Clare, ...	85 13 2	248 9 0	
„ Cork, ...	80 16 0	1,508 3 11	
„ Galway, ...	36 12 1	1,992 17 5	
„ Kerry, ...	496 17 0	974 0 0	
„ Limerick, . . .	119 5 10	41 1 5	
„ Mayo, ...	59 9 3	1,404 4 7	
„ Sligo, ...	59 19 2	394 18 2	
„ Leitrim, . . .	59 8 1	—	
„ Roscommon, . .	187 15 1	93 7 5	
„ Tipperary, . .	145 4 8	—	
	1,336 0 4	6,653 1 11	
			7,989 2 3
10. SEA AND COAST FISHERIES LOAN FUND, 47 & 48 Vic., c. 21 :—			
Repayments, ...	—	5,526 12 8	
Sale of Stock, ...	—	1,984 0 10	
Dividends on Stock, &c., . .	—	596 2 6	
			8,106 16 0
11. KINSALE HARBOUR :—			
Loan, ...	—	—	3,000 0 0
12. ARKLOW HARBOUR—"MAINTENANCE" :—			
Dues, ...	—	—	215 5 11
13. CLARE SLOB RECLAMATION :—			
Loan, ...	—	1,500 0 0	
Rent, &c., ...	—	46 15 9	
			1,546 15 9
14. GALWAY HARBOUR RECEIVER'S ACCOUNT :—			
Dues, ...	—	—	3,129 5 9
15. SOUTHERN RAILWAY :—			
Net Revenue for year ending 31st December, 1888,	—	3,346 2 11	
Amount received for payment of Baronial Guaranteed Dividends, . . .	—	3,145 0 0	
			6,491 2 11
Carried forward, . . .	—	—	65,979 2 1

of Public Works in the Year ended 31st March, 1889.

SERVICES—continued.

EXPENDITURE—continued.				£ s. d.	£ s. d.	£ s. d.
Brought forward,	.	.		—	—	38,711 8 4
9. Irish Reproductive Loan Fund, 37 & 38 Vic., c. 84, &c. :—			Purchase of Stock.	Advances.	Law Costs.	
County Clare,	.	.	—	363 0 0	7 16 8	
„ Cork,	.	.	—	1,955 9 10	11 19 3	
„ Galway,	.	.	2,644 16 3	1,265 10 0	91 19 9	
„ Kerry,	.	.	645 12 3	660 10 0	33 16 1	
„ Limerick,	.	.	—	6 10 0	—	
„ Mayo,	.	.	—	783 10 0	88 9 4	
„ Sligo,	.	.	—	169 0 0	23 15 7	
„ Leitrim,	.	.	198 8 1	—	—	
„ Roscommon,	.	.	596 4 3	—	—	
„ Tipperary,	.	.	—	1,000 0 0	—	
			3,984 0 10	6,302 9 10	253 16 2	10,440 6 10
10. Sea and Coast Fisheries Loan Fund, 47 & 48 Vic., c. 21 :—						
Loans to Fishermen,	.	.		—	6,441 16 0	
Law Costs, &c.,	.	.		—	33 16 5	6,475 12 3
11. Kinsale Harbour :—						
Purchase of Premises,	.	.		—	400 0 0	
Contract, Labour, &c.,	.	.		—	58 4 0	
Law Costs,	.	.		—	80 17 11	539 1 11
12. Arklow Harbour—"Maintenance" :—						
Superintendence and Repairs,	.	..		—	—	217 13 3
13. Clare Slob Reclamation :—						
Labour, Superintendence, &c.,	.	.		—	—	1,730 16 2
14. Galway Harbour Receiver's Account :—						
Repayment of Loan,	.	.		—	922 0 0	
Erection of Lock Gates, Dredging, Maintenance, &c.,	.		—	3,578 1 10	4,500 1 10
15. Southern Railway :—						
Payment of Interest on Loan,	.	.		—	1,800 0 0	
General Expenses of Management,	.	.		—	1,617 17 3	
Dividends, Income Tax, &c., paid on Baronial Guaranteed Stock,	.	.		—	3,145 0 0	6,562 17 3
Carried forward,	.	:		—	—	59,178 2 8

An Account showing the Receipts and Expenditure of the Commissioners

MISCELLANEOUS

RECEIPTS—continued.	£	s.	d.	£	s.	d.	£	s.	d.
Brought forward, . .	—			—			65,979	2	1
16. LEITRIM RENT RAILWAY:—									
On Account of Revenue for year ending 31st December, 1887, ...	—			402	10	8			
Net Revenue for year ended 31st December, 1888, .				1,681	3	11	2,083	14	7
17. EMIGRATION GRANTS :—									
18. SUNDRY ACCOUNTS :—									
Curragh of Kildare, ...	—			51	15	0			
Loans Insurance, ...	—			533	17	4			
Income Tax, ...	—			641	7	1			
Land Commission (Church Property) Office, .	—			600	0	0			
Insurance by Contractor of New Science and Art Buildings,	—			25	0	0			
House of Industry Hospitals, .	—			1	3	6			
Reps. of Hugh Kelly, Labourers Dwellings Loan Receivers Account, ...	—			37	2	10			
Island Bridge Waterworks, . . .	—			25	15	11			
Board of Admiralty, . . .	—			30	7	5			
Board of Trade, . . .	—			179	16	4			
Drainage Works, Closing Account, .	—			11	3	6			
Dividends on Stock lodged as Contractors' security,	—			7	3	6			
Temporary Receipts, . . .	—			4,645	9	7	6,780	1	0
							74,842	17	8

Office of Public Works, Dublin, 30th April, 1889.

of Public Works in the year ended 31st March, 1889.

SERVICES—continued.

EXPENDITURE—continued.	£ s. d.	£ s. d.	£ s. d.
Brought forward, . .	—	—	59,178 2 8
16. LETTERKENNY RAILWAY :—			
General Expenses of Management, . . .	—	442 9 8	
Interest on Loan—on account of, . . .	—	1,900 0 0	
			2,342 9 8
17. EMIGRATION GRANTS :—			
Grant to Swinford Poor Law Union, . .	—	—	40 0 0
18. SUNDRY ACCOUNTS :—			
Curragh of Kildare, . . .	—	51 15 0	
Lease Insurance, . . .	—	541 11 5	
Income Tax, . . .	—	631 5 10	
Land Commission (Church Property) Office, .	—	751 13 8	
Insurance by Contractor of new Science and Art Buildings,	—	1 11 3	
Island Bridge Waterworks, . . .	—	6 9 0	
Board of Admiralty, . . .	—	17 15 9	
Board of Trade, . . .	—	204 15 4	
Drainage Works Closing Account, . .	—	0 8 2	
Dividends on Stock, lodged as Contractors' Security,	—	7 3 6	
Temporary Receipts, . . .	—	905 5 10	
			3,199 16 9
			64,660 7 1
Balance, . . .	—	—	10,182 10 7
			74,842 17 8

Geo Pirrie, Accountant.

(A 8.) ARTERIAL DRAINAGE.—
These Works are executed by District Boards in

SCHEDULE.—ABSTRACT of FINAL AWARDS, and Repayments

Districts.	Counties.	Date when Award made final.	Area of Flooded or Injured Lands, which have been Drained or Improved	Cost per Acre of the Drainage, including Interest, &c.	Increase in the Annual Letting Value of these Lands, caused by Drainage.	Amount of Instalments payable half-yearly, to repay Cost and Interest, after deducting Redemptions.	
Ashboy River,	Meath,	4th April, 1869,	1,286	3 0	589	356	44
Ballinamorty,	Limerick,	2nd Oct., 1874,	179	7 1	62	32	20
Ballyadams,	Queen's,	9th Oct., 1882,	833	4 5	204	89	44
Ballysacarrig,	King's and Queen's,	9th April, 1882,	3,002	2 7	616	184	44
Ballyteigue & Kilmore,	Wexford,	9th Oct., 1886,	3,732	3 9	1,335	342	70
Baltrasny,	Kildare,	13th Mar., 1875,	1,955	4 0	866	204	44
Barnakyle,	Limerick,	3rd April, 1883,	1,017	9 15	607	240	44
Boolnarrig,	King's,	27th Mar., 1876,	925	8 7	197	89	20
Brickey River,	Waterford,	30th Sept., 1876,	829	5 4	297	129	30
Brida River,	Cork,	9th Oct., 1882,	1,209	6 15	531	214	70
Camoge,	Limerick,	25th Sept., 1876,	1,200	9 3	577	288	70
Clodiagh River,	Tipperary,	30th May, 1873,	1,857	4 3	688	212	44
Connell,	Kildare,	19th Jan., 1876,	747	6 6	171	77	20
Currygrane,	Longford,	9th Oct., 1882,	114	5 9	77	16	20
Derrinlough,	King's,	9th Oct., 1874,	623	3 6	143	61	44
Doohyle,	Limerick,	9th Oct., 1871,	609	6 7	146	71	20
Douglas River,	Carlow,	31st Mar., 1875,	3,028	4 7	929	425	44
Elphin,	Roscommon,	29th Mar., 1872,	2,393	6 11	1,036	489	44
Follistown,	Meath,	9th Oct., 1882,	888	5 2	59	26	44
Frankford River,	King's,	27th Mar., 1875,	1,294	6 5	416	204	20
Do.,	Do.,	4th April, 1884,				44	24
Garristown and Delvin,	Meath and Dublin,	3rd April, 1882,	3,222	1 9	461	146	90
Gully,	Queen's,	4th Oct., 1873,	1,034	4 11	242	142	44
Gully Upper,	Do.,	14th Mar., 1875,	506	4 12	129	49	70
Hogans Pass,	Tipperary,	9th Oct., 1882,	655	5 13	298	131	70
Inny, Upper,	Meath, Westmeath, Longford, & Cavan,	4th April, 1881,	11,675	7 3	3,790	3,147	70
Island Lakes and Glore River,	Mayo,	2nd April, 1875,	1,487	5 10	445	208	70
Kildare,	Kildare,	29th Sept., 1877,	2,247	3 11	505	111	20
Kilmastulla,	Tipperary,	30th July, 1870,	1,881	6 10	592	313	44
Larnon,	Meath,	3rd April, 1882,	879	7 0	204	154	70
Lerr River,	Kildare and Carlow,	9th Oct., 1882,	1,684	16 8	636	692	70
Lough Oughter,	Cavan,	4th April, 1876,	3,077	3 1	845	395	70
Milford,	Cork,	9th Oct., 1897,	1,915	8 14	499	221	70
Morning Star, Upper,	Limerick,	4th April, 1882,	839	3 13	356	179	70
Mulkear River,	Limerick,	20th Sept., 1877,	3,250	9 4	923	732	70
Nanny River,	Meath,	4th April, 1882,	734	10 5	585	201	70
Do., Upper,	Do.,	4th April, 1882,	163	6 7	72	26	70
Owveoroe,	Do.,	4th April, 1882,	2,207	6 0	861	279	70
Parsonstown,	Tipperary and King's,	25th Sept., 1874,	2,719	4 4	650	265	70
Quinagh,	Carlow,	19th Jan., 1876,	688	3 13	308	21	44
Rathangan River,	Kildare,	4th April, 1882,	6,984	3 12	3,044	1,640	70
Rathdowney,	Queen's,	9th Oct., 1882,	413	6 8	189	34	44
Silver River,	King's & Westmeath,	9th Oct., 1870,	1,802	3 13	215	123	44
Sixmilebridge,	Clare,	4th April, 1871,	2,585	7 13	1,329	611	30
Stoneyford River,	Kildare,	9th Oct., 1884,	3,384	6 15	1,550	731	70
Swanlinbar,	Cavan,	23rd Mar., 1880,	305	7 6	133	63	44
Swilly Burn,	Donegal,	9th Oct., 1884,	1,464	6 2	485	115	70
Torrent River,	Tyrone,	3rd April, 1875,	453	11 7	298	42	30
Tory Hill,	Limerick,	3rd April, 1872,	991	6 4	434	186	20
Ward River,	Dublin and Meath,	4th April, 1883,	688	7 10	314	186	70
[Continued on next page.]		Total,	87,904	3 4	28,022	14,182	—

a These charges have expired.

26 & 27 Vic., c. 88, &c.

accordance with the Provisions of the above Acts.

thereon, for the Year ended 31st March, 1889.

Total Amount Advanced, including interest to date of Award.	Portion of Total Advances charged to Counties for Public Works or refunded by Drainage Board.	Amount charged on Lands.	Repayments.			Districts.
			To 31st March, 1888.	Per year ended 31st March, 1889.	Total.	
£ s. d.	£ s. d.	£ s. d.	£ s. d.	£ s. d.	£ s. d.	
11,141 16 2	–	11,141 16 2	13,388 9 9	736 3 7	14,150 3 9	Athboy River.
1,286 3 10	–	1,288 3 10	1,135 3 4	65 16 8	1,201 0 0	Ballinasurry.
3,660 8 0	80 10 0	3,470 18 0	888 14 0	179 11 0	982 5 0	Ballydarre.
8,975 9 1	–	8,975 9 1	7,343 12 11	368 16 6	7,712 9 5	Ballynacarrig.
13,741 5 0	–	13,741 5 0	–	–	–	Ballytaigue and Kilmore.
8,211 1 2	330 13 9	7,880 8 0	5,902 2 6	1,163 11 8	8,084 14 9	Baltrasey.
8,186 17 8	°609 18 7	7,577 5 2	2,737 19 10	475 7 10	3,214 7 8	Barnakyle.
2,350 0 0	–	2,350 0 0	275 4 6	68 19 1	344 3 1	Do.
3,107 2 4	–	3,107 2 4	2,558 15 9	215 8 6	2,773 19 3	Boolnacrig.
4,923 12 0	–	4,283 12 0	4,710 14 5	258 15 2	4,969 18 7	Brickey River.
8,721 5 3	106 9 5	8,615 5 9	3,206 5 4	264 2 0	3,471 7 4	Bride River.
11,745 19 6	200 0 0	11,545 19 6	6,329 7 6	376 8 6	6,706 17 6	Camoge.
6,938 11 6	–	6,938 11 6	7,117 11 6	493 15 8	7,610 8 6	Clodiagh River.
2,482 12 0	–	2,480 12 6	2,905 18 0	134 3 1	3,049 16 1	Connell.
628 15 0	–	628 15 0	175 14 5	20 14 6	196 8 11	Currygrane.
3,105 12 9	40 0 0	3,065 12 9	1,880 3 6	156 12 2	1,936 15 8	Derrialough.
2,513 6 0	–	2,513 6 0	1,584 10 11	56 10 10	1,641 1 9	Deshyle.
18,663 8 8	190 0 0	13,473 8 8	11,530 3 6	643 4 5	12,173 7 11	Douglas River.
15,940 17 0	488 0 0	15,452 17 6	18,900 10 7	825 16 2	10,726 6 9	Ephin.
1,051 12 0	–	1,051 12 6	–	–	–	Fellstown.
4,746 5 4	80 0 0	4,666 5 4	4,088 10 8	441 3 2	3,529 13 10	Frankford River
575 17 4	–	575 17 4	239 7 6	50 4 5	289 10 9	Do.
4,948 15 0	225 0 0	4,723 15 0	2,103 3 4	340 16 10	2,443 0 2	Garristown and Delvin.
4,517 11 6	–	4,517 11 6	4,971 0 5	294 2 10	4,565 5 3	Gully.
2,447 15 9	70 0 0	2,377 15 2	1,363 17 2	606 11 10	1,757 9 0	Gully, Upper.
5,256 12 0	214 4 0 / °300 0 0	4,642 8 6	716 8 1	223 16 4	937 4 5	Hagan's Pass.
91,606 5 6	3,102 18 6 / °3,750 0 0	86,585 12 0	32,294 14 0	4,870 11 3	37,175 3 3	Inny, Upper.
8,704 19 7	213 6 0 / °180 0 0	8,399 13 7	5,217 17 11	602 6 3	5,820 2 2	Island Lakes and Glore River.
5,857 4 6	290 0 0	5,597 4 6	5,672 11 1	393 8 6	5,075 19 1	Kildare.
10,969 7 8	–	10,969 7 8	12,374 12 8	611 8 10	13,986 1 6	Kilmastulla.
6,217 12 10	35 15 4	6,181 17 6	3,388 7 10	299 5 0	3,617 12 10	Larecor.
37,916 9 0	200 0 0	37,714 9 0	2,792 1 10	1,373 13 8	4,065 16 6	Larr River.
16,188 4 0	–	16,188 4 0	7,685 13 9	960 12 6	8,649 6 3	Lough Oughter.
8,571 14 6	–	8,571 14 6	–	362 3 0	362 3 0	Milford.
7,425 0 0	250 0 0	7,175 0 0	250 0 0	167 6 11	357 6 11	Morning Star, Upper.
30,779 0 0	364 1 0 / 544 0 0	29,914 19 0	14,604 15 6	2,842 18 0	17,347 13 8	Mulkear River.
8,642 5 7	°70 19 7	8,648 6 0	70 19 7	731 15 7	802 15 2	Nanny River.
1,043 12 6	–	1,043 19 6	–	26 1 10	26 1 10	Do. Upper.
11,668 12 6	346 16 5	11,121 16 9	–	294 3 9	294 3 9	Owenroe.
11,699 17 1	150 0 0	11,549 17 1	7,816 18 1	505 1 0	8,316 19 1	Parsonstown.
2,700 13 8	°200 0 0	2,500 13 8	3,072 0 8	213 11 6	3,285 12 2	Qsinagh.
77,507 6 0	1,185 0 0	76,622 6 9	26,634 9 8	2,949 11 9	29,584 1 5	Rathangan River.
2,645 6 3	–	2,645 6 3	3,635 15 1	190 2 10	3,625 17 11	Rathdowney.
5,971 2 9	–	5,071 9 0	4,516 13 0	257 13 0	4,776 8 0	Silver River.
20,829 15 11	624 1 8	19,904 13 3	21,780 14 2	1,282 11 10	22,963 6 0	Sixmilebridge.
32,230 0 0	1,645 11 10 / °600 0 0	29,984 8 2	7,530 10 3	1,629 5 1	8,769 15 4	Stoneyford River.
2,089 5 6	143 0 0	1,960 5 6	1,139 19 0	137 17 0	1,277 9 0	Swanlinbar.
9,230 13 5	637 18 9 / °14 0 5	8,578 14 0	1,040 7 4	4,332 14 7	5,573 1 11	Swilly Burn.
5,332 1 6	187 10 0	5,144 11 6	4,560 16 1	327 15 6	4,888 11 7	Torrent River.
6,110 13 8	–	6,110 13 8	3,620 5 8	459 1 2	3,879 7 0	Tory Hill
6,845 17 9	196 19 0	6,648 18 9	1,606 5 4	357 3 6	1,963 9 0	Ward River.
870,680 5 3 / f 2,350 0 0	17,196 12 1	855,631 15 2	273,751 18 0	34,174 6 11	308,905 4 11	

f Issued out of the Irish Church Fund   ° Refunded by Drainage Board, being portion of advances not expended.

(A 8.) ARTERIAL DRAINAGE.—

These Works are executed by District Boards in

ARTERIAL DRAINAGE WORKS in progress

Districts.	Counties.	Date when Awards made final.	Area of Flooded or Injured Lands, which have been Drained or Improved, Statute Measure.	Cost per Acre of the Drainage, including Interest, &c.	Increase in the Annual Letting Value of these Lands, caused by Drainage.	Amount of Instalments payable half-yearly, to repay Cost, with Interest, after deducting Redemptions.	Number of half-yearly Instalments to repay principal and interest.
			A. R. P.	£ s. d.	£ s. d.	£ s. d.	
From preceding page,		–	–	–	–	14,182 11 8	–
Ballycollihoe,	Tipperary,	–	–	–	–	–	–
Cashen River,	Kerry,	–	–	–	–	–	–
Glashoue,	Cork,	–	–	–	–	–	–
Gananagh,	Limerick,	–	–	–	–	–	–
Killard,	Cork,	–	–	–	–	–	–
Lough Erne,	Fermanagh, Cavan, Monaghan, and Donegal,	–	–	–	–	–	–
Do. (Navigation),	Do.,	–	–	–	–	550 6 6 60	
River Suck,	Roscommon & Galway,	–	–	–	–	–	
Total charge against districts,		–	–	–	–	14,732 17 8	–

Office of Public Works, Dublin, 30th April, 1889.

26 & 27 Vic., c. 88, &c.

accordance with the Provisions of the above Acts.

showing the Issues made to 31st March, 1889.

Total Amount advanced, including Interest, to Date of Award.	Portion of Total Advanced charged to Counties for Public Works, or refunded by Drainage Board.	Amount charged on Lands.	Repayments.			Districts.
			To 31st March, 1888.	For year ended 31st March, 1889.	Total.	
£ s. d.	£ s. d.	£ s. d.	£ s. d.	£ s. d.	£ s. d.	
{ 270,480 5 2 / 2,550 0 0 }	} 17,196 19 1	—	275,73: 15 0	34,174 6 11	309,906 4 11	
293 0 0	—	—	—	—	—	Ballycollton.
6,648 0 0	—	—	—	—	—	Cashen River.
1,802 0 0	—	—	—	—	—	Glasheen.
10,008 0 0	—	—	—	461 0 0	461 0 0	Greenagh.
300 0 0	—	—	—	—	—	Killard.
147,080 0 0	—	—	—	—	—	Lough Erne.
17,197 14 0	17,197 14 0	—	1,103 19 10	1,035 0 5	2,135 13 3	Do.
{ 85,600 0 0 { /3,786 1 0 }	} —	—	—	—	—	River Suck.
535,173 2 5 /6,136 1 0						
544,309 3 3	34,396 6 1	—	276,838 16 10	35,670 7 4	312,509 16 9	

/ Issued out of the Church Fund.

Geo. Perris, *Accountant.*

APPENDIX B.

LAND IMPROVEMENT.—EXTRACTS FROM INSPECTORS' REPORTS.

MR. F. COFFEE, for KILKENNY, WATERFORD, and parts of TIPPERARY.

Owing to the fact of many tenants being still in arrear of rent, they are for the present deterred from improving their holdings or availing themselves of the borrowing powers under the statute, pending a settlement of their arrears and future rents. When leaseholders' rents are judicially fixed by the Land Commission Courts under the Land Law Act, 1887, with a liberal extension of peasant proprietors under the Ashbourne Act, I feel very little doubt of an extension of loan operations under the Land Improvement and Land Law Acts.

MR. C. G. ORMSBY, for parts of SLIGO, ROSCOMMON, MAYO, and GALWAY.

With regard to the class of works in progress, they are much the same as heretofore, viz.—drainage, fencing, and building; but there is, I believe, a decided improvement in the quality of the work now being done under Section 31 of the Land Law Act.

MR. A. BARBY, for parts of SLIGO and ROSCOMMON and LEITRIM.

The superior character of the applicants and the more permanent nature of the works proposed, i.e., building and thorough drainage instead of open drainage, also appears well marked.

Again, there appears a strong tendency amongst those who purchased their holdings to further enhance their value by loans for improvement.

MR. H. BRETT for parts of KING'S, QUEEN'S, and TIPPERARY.

There appears also amongst the newer borrowers a desire to expend their loans to the greater permanent advantage of their holdings.

MR. J. W. MURRAY, for WESTMEATH, LONGFORD, and part of MEATH and KING'S COUNTY.

That these loans have in many instances induced the borrower to carry out further improvements on his farm after the loan has been closed I can testify to, and in the case of drainage, the fact of a neighbour having improved his lands, has suggested to the adjoining tenant to carry out some such work on his own farm.

MR. A. HADE, for CARLOW, WEXFORD, and parts of KILDARE, WICKLOW and QUEEN'S.

In most cases the value of work executed under and in connection with the loans exceeded—in some cases greatly exceeded—the amount borrowed, thereby increasing the security for repayment.

MR. W. G. KELLY, for parts of GALWAY and MAYO.

I can perceive a strong, progressive desire on the part of the occupiers, now that they have fixity of tenure, to improve their holdings, and they are beginning to recognise the great advantage of being able to borrow money for this purpose at a low rate of interest. I find that by far the best work is done by the tenants who have purchased their holdings. Others will not apply for an instalment when in arrear with their rent. Some small farmers who carry out all the works by their own or sons' labour complain of the short time allowed for the completion of the works, as they have their farm work to attend to as well, but as an extension of time is generally allowed, when necessary, I would suggest no alterations in the rules

MR. E. LYNAM, for parts of GALWAY and ROSCOMMON.

Owing to the strained relations between landlords and tenants on several large properties situated in my district, applications for loans have been impossible but I am happy to state, from my own observation, and from conversations with farmers, landlords, and others, that the country shows decided signs of improvement. This will certainly give rise to an increase in applications for loans. In general I find that where a loan has been carried out, the borrower has gone on improving his farm after the final certificate has been given, and the loan closed. The slating of dwelling-houses and offices is a great improvement. It elevates the moral status of the farmer—conduces considerably to health and cleanly habits, and saves the straw for his manure-heap. Drainage generally increases the value of the farm enormously—prevents losses through disease in sheep, &c., and good division and rearing fences leave the farmer time to till his soil instead of chasing his own and his neighbour's stock.

MR. A. R. WILKINSON, for the larger parts of CORK.

I notice that in most cases borrowers seem inclined to carry out their work better than was formerly the case, and there appears to be a tendency now to borrow more for building than for land reclamation, many tenants apparently being able to do the latter work themselves, year by year, and only borrowing where a sum of ready money becomes necessary. Also there appears to be a spirit of greater contentment among the tenant-farmers recently. Many also express a wish to borrow for improvement, but are waiting in the hope of an extension of the Purchase Acts, as they think they may then be able to borrow on more favourable terms.

MR. A. IRWIN, for parts of LIMERICK and CORK.

I am sure where purchases take place under Lord Ashbourne's Act, that loans will be applied for immediately. Several instances of this have taken place in my district. The applications for loans have increased considerably of late in my district.

APPENDIX C.

KINGSTOWN HARBOUR

SUMMARY of RAINFALL and TIDAL OBSERVATIONS.

Month.	Fall in inches during month.	Maximum in 24 Hours.		Number of days on which rain fell.	Maximum at High Water.			Minimum at Low Water.		
		Date.	Fall in inches.		Date.	Height.	Wind.	Date.	Height.	Wind.
1888.						a. h.			a. h.	
April,	1·49	12	·43	12	27	13 6	N.W.	26	−1 6	S.E.
May,	1·64	30	·37	6	27	12 0	E.	26	−1 0	S.E.
June,	0·71	26	·21	14	24	11 9	N.E.	13	−0 6	N.
July,	4·11	26	·46	16	26	12 3	S.	10	+0 6	N.W.
August,	1·73	26	·25	12	24	12 0	S.	9	+0 6	S.E.
September,	·99	26	·25	4	6	11 3	N.W.	6	−1 0	N.W.
October,	1·12	2	·24	11	6	12 0	N.W.	8	−1 0	N.W.
November,	3·04	11	·70	24	3	12 9	S.E.	3	+0 6	N.E.
December,	3·80	30	1·52	17	3	13 6	S.W.	31	+1 3	S.W.
1889.										
January,	3·49	2	1·65	12	30	12 3	W.	21	+1 0	N.W.
February,	2·05	11	·57	11	1	13 0	N.W.	6	−1 6	N.W.
March,	1·39	30	·26	13	19	13 6	S.W.	30	ZERO.	W.N.W.

RETURN OF VESSELS USING KINGSTOWN HARBOUR.

	1885–1886.		1886–1887.		1887–1888.		1888–1889.	
	Number.	Tonnage.	Number.	Tonnage.	Number.	Tonnage.	Number.	Tonnage.
Home Trade.								
Trading Vessels,	657	77,417	632	62,960	551	51,948	385	43,750
Yachts,	96	7,373	54	4,854	52	5,678	99	6,563
Trawlers and Fishing Vessels,	1,518	66,770	883	34,883	40	—	40	35
Steam Vessels,	84	19,092	70	12,753	52	33,156	72	15,119
„ Yachts,	48	13,537	38	7,920	26	6,554	36	2,572
Belonging to Port, Yachts, Pilots, &c.,	33	460	76	220	22	—	12	60
Foreign Trade.								
Sailing Vessels,	18	22,584	21	22,893	17	12,772	13	9,368
Steam Vessels,	2	954	10	6,423	4	2,146	1	455
Man-of-War and Troopships, Store Ships, and H. M's. Yachts,	26	—	—	—	22	57,344	9	22,500